FICTION BLURBS THE BEST PAGE FORWARD WAY

THE STEP-BY-STEP GUIDE TO WIN OVER READERS, SELL MORE BOOKS, AND MARKET LIKE A PRO

PHOEBE J. RAVENCRAFT

BRYAN COHEN

FOREWORD

In 2015, I started writing book descriptions for the author community. My side project turned into a company called Best Page Forward. After writing hundreds of these blurbs myself, I began to hire writers who I could teach the process so we could help more people. But despite this fact, when my daughter was born in late 2016, I continued to write, edit, or look over every single description we worked on. As our company grew, so did my responsibilities with my time and energy shrinking every day.

When 2018 rolled around, I knew that I would have to fully hand off the writing reins. That's when something wholly unexpected happened: the blurbs got better and the process started to evolve. With over 5,000 descriptions written by the start of 2022, we'd transformed our own method so much that our first book on the subject (*How to Write a Sizzling Synopsis*) now only scratched the surface of how to write a solid description.

Phoebe Ravencraft, an author in her own right, has played a major part in shaping the development of our writers. As the Editor-in-Chief of Best Page Forward, she has now edited more descriptions than I ever had. She's the best person to teach you our up-to-date process.

After writing the book, my team and I wondered if we'll actually put ourselves out of the blurb-writing business by sharing our workflow from beginning to end. But we'll take that risk in service of helping the amazing author community to move forward.

I hope you enjoy the book and that it helps your blurbs immensely. Thank you for your incredible support!

Sincerely,

Bryan Cohen

CEO, Best Page Forward

CHAPTER 1

THE BEST PAGE FORWARD WAY

I used to think I was pretty good at book descriptions. I'd been writing marketing copy of one variety or another since launching my first business in 1996. I have a gift for clever turns of phrase, and I've studied marketing, selling, public relations, and consumer psychology *a lot*. After having written back-cover copy for several employers in the games-publishing business, as well as a ton of my own books after launching an indie-author career, I was confident I knew what I was doing.

Then I met this guy, Bryan Cohen. I knew him by reputation, and I'd bought a couple of his courses under his Selling for Authors banner. But we met for the first time at the Sell More Books Show Summit in May of 2018. We chatted between presentations a few times, and needing work, I proposed maybe coming to write for him at his ad copy agency, Best Page Forward. He told me he'd been thinking of expanding his staff to keep up with demand. He said he'd let me know.

So, when he announced a month or two later that he was looking to hire some copywriters, I applied. And I was good enough to make it through the process. In September of 2018, I joined the BPF team as a first draft writer.

And then everything got incredibly hard.

Maybe I was a good copywriter before. Maybe I was just fooling myself. But I was *not* good by BPF standards when I first began work. My trainer, Abigail Dunard (whom I would later join as the co-host of the *Blurbs Sell Books* podcast) was both kind and patient. My first editor was Claire Taylor, who would go on to found FFS Media and the excellent Supercharge Your Story/Series courses. To his credit, Bryan never made me feel like an idiot (although I felt that way... a lot).

These folks and a few others (notably Robert Scanlon) taught me the Best Page Forward Way. Thankfully, they kept after me until I got it. I realized that, no matter how good I had been at writing book descriptions before, I could be better. There was a superior means to do it. A proven, results-oriented system that leveled the playing field for indie authors against trad houses and increased sales conversion.

Three years later, I'm Best Page Forward's Editor-in-Chief. I've personally worked on over a thousand blurbs, and I edit several a day. I also get to teach this amazing system to our writers and help them improve their craft.

Now, I'm so excited to be able to share it with you.

Most authors *hate* writing book descriptions. They don't know what needs to be in them. They don't know how long they should be. And they can't understand why it's so damned hard to write a 200-word blurb when they just wrote a 75,000-word novel.

My goal is to make it easier. The system outlined in this book is how Best Page Forward has helped hundreds of authors convince readers to buy their work. I'm going to walk you through it from beginning to end, so that by the time you finish (and have done the exercises that will help you learn it), you'll feel comfortable and confident writing blurbs. Maybe you won't love it. But hopefully, you won't hate it. Hopefully, it won't fill you with dread.

Bryan Cohen and his team of experts made me a better blurb writer. Read on and apply these concepts, and we'll do the same for you.

. . .

Organization

I've organized the book into two main sections. In the first, we'll discuss blurb theory – the science and basic concepts you need to understand to craft compelling copy. In the second, I will take you step-by-step through the exact structure of a Best Page Forward description. We'll examine precisely how to build a blurb with one or two POV characters, and I'll also cover how to write a description for a memoir or other narrative nonfiction. We'll zoom in with an entire chapter dedicated to each sentence in the blurb, so you'll really understand what it's supposed to do and how to write it. There is also a chapter on advanced techniques after you get your feet under you.

My goal was to make this the most thorough book on how to write a blurb available. However, keep in mind that the subject matter is confined to novels and narrative nonfiction like memoirs. If you've written a self-help book or a how-to manual, this is not the book for you. Nonfiction has a separate set of concerns and the blurbs to sell them work differently.

Methodology

Before we get into a deep discussion on how to pen a fantastic fiction blurb, I want to talk about how we're approaching the topic.

First and most importantly, I need you to let go of any preconceived notions you may have about book descriptions. When Bryan Cohen founded Best Page Forward in 2015, he was already an ace copywriter, having freelanced prolifically for multiple companies. At the time of this writing, BPF has been in business for six years, and we have written descriptions for over 5,000 books over every conceivable genre. In that time, our process has continued to evolve since Bryan published *How to Write a Sizzling Synopsis* in 2016 and since I joined the company two years later. As a result, we've gotten better at our craft as we've discovered what really sells books.

Some of the concepts you'll learn in this book may surprise you. They may fly in the face of things you've been told or taught. But in our experience, they work.

Publishing is a hard business. Success can be elusive. And independent authors cannot play the game the same way trad authors, especially well-known successful ones, do.

But the good news is you *can* be hugely profitable as an indie. We've found that our techniques help make that possible. So, I hope you'll trust the system you're about to learn.

In addition to the Best Page Forward Way perhaps being different than what you'd expect, I also approach teaching it in a manner you might find unusual. I'll confess right now to having majored in English. I spent years learning to analyze story structure, and while that hasn't proven especially helpful in terms of finding work, it drives how I approach looking at a novel's synopsis and determining what parts will sell it. As we go through both blurb theory and structure, I'll be discussing the elements of fiction as they relate to crafting good sales copy.

I'm also a member of the last generation of children forced to diagram sentences in school. Don't worry, I won't inflict that on you. But it really helped me understand parts of speech and sentence structure. I discuss those ideas in-depth because you need to see how to choose the best words and expressions for your blurbs.

I do all this because I'm a big believer in the idea that mastering a skill occurs when you understand the reasoning behind it. Writing effective book descriptions is not easy. If I can help you learn it by drawing back the curtains of story structure and grammar so that you can really see how the moving parts work, I'm all for it.

Finally, I believe in teaching by example and in learning by doing. Throughout the book, I'll be offering sample phrases, sentences, and paragraphs. For many of these, I draw on pop culture. I'll write sentences as though I were assigned to do a fiction blurb for a famous movie or novel. I've tried to choose ones that the majority of us have seen or read so that there will be a familiarity that makes teaching the concepts easier. I went as broadly as possible, choosing films and occasionally novels in as many different genres as I could. Hopefully, that will help you grasp the concepts more readily.

There will also be homework. You may be groaning about that but take heart. The exercises aren't hard. If you're going to learn to write blurbs, you'll need to practice the concepts in the book. As I noted above, writing effective sales copy isn't easy. There's no one trick I can teach you to make it all come simply. Remember that I wasn't as good at this as I had thought when I first started at BPF. But by practicing, you'll be able to develop the skill necessary to write more effective book descriptions.

For the best results, I recommend doing the exercises as soon as you finish the chapter in which they appear. That way, the lesson will be fresh in your mind. But I understand that some people learn best by taking in all the information before trying to do the work, and you might be reading this book on your commute, in line at the grocery store, or some other place where you can't just whip out your notebook and practice writing a book description. You'll get the most out of the instruction if you do the homework. But do it when and where it works best for you. All the exercises are collected in Appendix B for your convenience.

So ... are you excited? Are you ready to learn a craft that will help you sell more books and maybe make your author dreams come true? Then let's dive into the theory behind our fantastic fiction blurbs!

CHAPTER 2
WHAT'S A BLURB?

So, what exactly *is* a blurb? What does it do? Why do you need one?

The word gets thrown around a lot, and everyone seems to think it means something different. Let's start with a basic definition to make sure we're all on the same page.

Terminology

Technically, a "blurb" is a recommendation from another author or expert. For example, if you were penning a horror novel, you might seek a blurb that went something like:

> *The most terrifying thing I have ever read. Scarier than* IT.
> --Stephen King

The idea behind this sort of thing was that another author expert saying something nice about your book lent it credibility and made people want to read it. After all, if Stephen King thinks it's good, it must be, right?

Thus, getting a blurb (or several) for your book was really helpful.

Well, language evolves over time. (You can decide for yourself whether that's good or bad.) With the advent of eBook publishing and the elimination of gatekeepers preventing aspiring authors from getting their work in front of readers, "blurb" came to be synonymous with the proper term for what it is: "book description."

A book description tells a potential buyer what sort of book this is, something about the plot, and why that person would enjoy it. It's also known as "back cover copy." Basically, it's a (hopefully) clever description of what the reader can expect to find inside.

In the days before indie publishing, book descriptions were written by an ad agency or by someone at the publishing house putting the book out into the world. Said individual likely had not read the book, probably had not received any training on writing effective book descriptions, and might not be good at ad copy in the first place. Authors had just about zero control over who wrote their book description and what was in it. Many authors hated their back cover copy.

Good news! As an indie author, you are not just the writer; you're also the publisher! That means you have total control over what goes into your book description. So, revel in it. And then freak out a little, because, OMG, you're responsible for getting it right.

Don't worry. We've got you covered!

Anyway, these days, "blurb" and "book description" mean pretty much the same thing. At Best Page Forward, we tend to use "blurb" more frequently for the sole reason that it's shorter and easier to say, let alone write. (Gotta love one-syllable words.)

One more term to get out of the way before we dive into what a blurb really does. In advertising parlance, "copy" is basically any piece of writing whose job is to sell something. Your book description is a piece of ad copy. So are any hooks you're using for Amazon ads. A movie or TV show tagline is ad copy. Anything you read on a billboard or print ad is copy. You get the idea.

"Copywriting" then, is the skill or activity of penning ad copy. And it is this particular skillset we're going to teach you herein.

A Blurb's Job

I'm about to reveal something radical, something that may make no sense to you. Ready?

Despite its name, the job of a book description is not to actually describe *your book.*

Let me repeat that so that we're absolutely clear: Despite its name, the job of a book description is not to actually *describe* your book.

Hopefully, that didn't totally blow your socks off, but if it did, go put them back on and then let's dig into what my radicalism is all about.

A book description is not a summary of your novel. Its job is not to tell the reader what happens in the book. Its purpose is not to describe the deep human themes and important truths it reveals. (I'm lookin' at you, lit-fic authors.) And its job is not to delve deeply into the plot, the myriad number of characters, or the books it compares favorably to. (More on that later.)

So many authors (and trad-house copywriters) make this mistake. But it's essential you understand this before we go any further. If you spend your time telling the reader all about what's inside, they will navigate away from your sales page and look for something else. Let go of the idea that you need to convince readers of the depth of the story and the extent of your genius. Your book description's job is not to do these things.

What *does* it do, then? It's really pretty simple:

A blurb's purpose is to sell your book.

Let that sink in for a moment. Think about it.

You may have become an author for a variety of reasons. Maybe you have stories in your head you just have to get out. Maybe you have something important you want to say. Maybe you saw other people making money at this publishing thang and decided you wanted a piece of the pie.

Whatever your motivation was for getting into this indie author biz, you share a goal with every other writer out there – wanting people to buy your book. Your blurb is the tool to make that happen. That's its whole purpose.

I'm going to teach you how to write one that will make it happen, no matter what genre of fiction you pen.

To do that, I need you to let go of your preconceptions. Tell yourself, "Yo, Self! I do not need to summarize my book to make it sell!" Internalize this message. It will help you craft really compelling book descriptions.

Because every decision you make will be designed to help sell your novel.

This is your philosophical foundation. We're grounding ourselves in sales strategy. In the next chapter, we'll take a look at the things your description must include to be successful.

Ready? Turn the page and let's dive in!

CHAPTER 3
ESSENTIAL ELEMENTS

Okay, now we understand what a blurb is and what it is supposed to do. So, if its job is *not* to summarize the book, what actually goes into it?

In this chapter, we're going to look at some key features your description must have to work. We're still going to be a bit zoomed out because these are big ideas. Don't worry. The nitty-gritty stuff is coming. But big ideas first.

Brevity

Your blurb needs to be short. This is one of the most essential concepts you need to get your mind around. In the twenty-first-century, internet age of "Ooh! Shiny!", you do not have time to explain the backstory, discuss the intricate details of the world in which your masterpiece is set, or spend time with each of the sixteen main characters in your ensemble cast. (I'm lookin' at you, sci-fi/fantasy authors.)

For good or ill, the modern human mind gets bored quickly. You've only got seconds to capture – and most importantly, *keep* – a reader's attention. To sell your novel, you need to have a brief, stimulating blurb that quickly hooks interest and proceeds swiftly to the call to action. (More on the call to action, or "CTA," later.)

At Best Page Forward, we aim for a blurb of about 200 to 250 words. We don't make that a hard line, but if the description is creeping close to 300 words, that's a pretty good indication that we're going on too long and need to cut something.

The last thing you want is buyers looking at your ad copy and thinking, "TL;DR." We want to give them enough that they are invested in finding out what happens but not so much they feel like they've read a mini version of the novel. Remember: A book description is not a summary.

Smooth Copy

Okay, here is another concept that may force you to abandon previous notions. The rules of proper English grammar do not apply to ad copy.

Please get comfortable with beginning a sentence with a coordinating conjunction.

Sentence fragments are okay.

Sometimes, skipping a comma is all right.

Listen, I get it. I am a total grammar nerd, and I'm really ... let's call it *fastidious* about my prose.

But ad copy is not prose. Indeed, it's closer to poetry. And just like with verse, you can take liberties with the rules to make it work.

However, being an effective copywriter does not amount to simply flipping off your eighth-grade English teacher and doing whatever you want. The rules of grammar exist for a reason: clarity. If your copy is unclear, that teacher you just gave the bird to is going to smirk behind their textbook as readers get confused and don't buy your novel.

And you wouldn't want to give that strict grammarian the satisfaction, would you?

You have to write with purpose. And the purpose – the job – of a blurb is to sell your novel. Breaking the rules is done in service to that mission.

You want punchy, clever turns of phrase. Don't write run-on sentences. Don't put in parenthetical phrases. Don't give us a bunch of technical terms. Just short, smooth, fun copy.

Here's an example of what I mean. Read the following sentence aloud, stopping to take a breath every time you see a comma or other piece of punctuation:

> *Isabelle, a banker with ten years of experience, was tired of all the career-oriented men she saw at work and conferences, and she just wanted someone nice, someone who made her feel safe.*

Did you feel how herky-jerky that was? It's a well-constructed compound sentence that is properly punctuated. But it keeps stopping and starting, and that forces the reader to restart the flow each time.

Every time that happens is an opportunity for distraction. If they are kicked out of the flow, a reader can be tempted to look away. If they do, there is every chance they'll go follow that new shiny thing they saw.

We have a rule at Best Page Forward: You're only allowed one comma per sentence, unless you're listing a set (in which case, the commas aid clarity). Now, that does not mean we just cut two of the commas from a sentence that would properly have three. It means, write the sentence so that you only *need* one comma. Why? It improves flow.

Think about that same sentence above. What if we rewrote this way:

> *Tired of all the career-oriented men she sees at work and conferences, Isabelle just wants someone who makes her feel safe.*

If you read that aloud, you no doubt noticed how much smoother it was. There's only one pause. It doesn't go on so long that your mind starts to get tired, and all the essential ideas are still there.

Likewise, we can reduce the break between sentences by starting with a conjunction. For example:

> *Tired of all the career-oriented men she sees at work and conferences, Isabelle just wants someone who makes her feel safe. So when her friends set her up with yet another guy in a power tie, she figures she'll have one quick drink and then ditch him. But she's stunned when the sexy-as-sin date confesses he dreams of a quiet life on his own ranch.*

Did you feel how easily those sentences flow together? They're joined neatly by conjunctions that allow the eye to slide smoothly from one to the next, keeping the mind engaged while still allowing for those critical pauses to breathe.

Dramatic Phrases

As important as it is to keep things flowing, we don't want to put readers to sleep either. We need to have some excitement to keep them engaged.

Look again at the example paragraph from above. Notice how I injected it with some drama by using dynamic words and phrases. Isabelle wants "someone who makes her feel safe." Her friends set her up with "another guy in a power tie." She plans to "ditch him." And our enigmatic man is "sexy-as-sin."

Those words and phrases all evoke images in our minds. Much like a poet, we're painting with words, drawing a picture for the reader. That's engaging. It gets the reader involved.

You can add drama with another tried-and-true copy technique, the sentence fragment. Consider this example:

> *And as the clock ticks down, Xander faces a terrible choice between clinging to his ideals or losing the love of his life. Forever.*

By breaking "forever" off into its own sentence, we added a metric ton of drama. Things are already bad by facing Xander with an awful choice. Yet we managed to ramp up the tension even further with that one-word sentence.

You'll see this technique used a lot in hooks and taglines. Often, a set of three is separated by being broken into three distinct sentences instead of simply divided by commas. For instance, we might write a hook for our sample description from above like this:

> *A woman seeking safety. A man with a dream. One last chance for real love.*

All three of those sentences are fragments. But they're short, impactful, and they up the drama by standing by themselves instead of being collected together.

Good ad copy sings. It flows from one sentence to the next, and it has plenty of drama to engage the mind and pull the reader in.

Even if it breaks the rules.

Character-Driven

Fiction is about characters. No matter what kind of story you've crafted, regardless of which genre you write, the novel revolves around a central figure and the conflict they face.

That means the main character has to be the focus of your blurb. Everything in your description should be driven by the MC, not the outside world, the supporting cast, or the terrifying events that are unfolding. Just like with the novel itself, your protagonist needs to carry the blurb.

Remember earlier in this chapter when I told you the description needed to be brief? That applies here. You may have an ensemble cast, but you need to pick one of them to be featured. You can't give them all their fair space. Focus on one. Choose the most-main character if there isn't a singular protagonist.

If you're writing a blurb for a romance novel, you can have two MC's. We need to know about each of the lovers and how they will come together. You can also do this if you have two equal leads.

But that's it. No more than two characters and only if it's absolutely necessary. As soon as you add a third "main" character to the description, you risk causing reader confusion as they try to keep track of who everyone is. The human mind can really only keep one or two new ideas straight at a time. Sometimes, it can handle three. Sometimes, that's too much.

We have a saying at Best Page Forward: The confused mind says no.

Don't risk confusing your readers with too many characters. They'll decide your book is too complex and go look for something easier to understand. By including info about fewer characters now, you'll be able to save these exciting reveals in the context of the entire story. This will be a better experience for your committed readers who've already purchased the book.

I'll discuss characters more in the next chapter. For now, figure out who your protagonist is and hang your blurb on their capable shoulders.

Stakes

The essence of fiction is conflict. To create conflict, you need to have something at stake. What does your MC stand to lose as a result of the action of the novel? What happens if they make a mistake?

Will someone get hurt?

Will they blow their last chance at romance?

Will they lose their job?

Will their family stop speaking to them?

Something has to be at stake for your protagonist, and we need to know what it is in the blurb. This risk, this fear of loss or danger, drives readers to find out what happens next. That's why it's helpful when you're trying to sell to them to let them know something could go wrong. You must convince them that this character they're growing to care for has a chance to fail.

Without stakes, you only have a series of vaguely related events. You are unlikely to have growth. Whether you write page-turning genre fiction or the Great American Novel, your readers want to know what's at stake for the protagonist.

We'll be discussing stakes throughout this book. They're absolutely critical to your blurb's success.

Point of View and Tense

Many authors ask us if the blurb they write should be in the same point of view and tense as their book. More often than not, the answer is actually no.

The great majority of book descriptions are written in third-person point of view and present tense.

Like in most aspects of marketing, we're often trying to meet reader expectations. And since traditional publishers have been using third-person blurbs for decades, that's what many readers expect to see. Simply put, when readers anticipate a certain thing in the marketing, you'd be wise to do it.

Now, what about the growing trend of first-person blurbs in certain romance subgenres?

We should absolutely pay attention to how trends change over time, but since most blurbs remain in third-person, that's what we'll focus on in the coming chapters.

Fortunately, since third-person descriptions are significantly easier to write than compelling first-person blurbs, this will end up being a blessing in disguise.

In the upcoming homework exercises, we recommend that you use third-person and present tense as you complete the assignments.

The Inciting Incident

As a professional blurb writer, the inciting incident is one of the most frustrating parts of my job. Why? Because so many authors don't actually know what it is. Let's clear up the mystery right away.

The inciting incident is the external event that forces the main character out of their initial emotional state or situation and into the action of the narrative.

What does that mean? Let's break it down.

First, the inciting incident is something external to our MC. It's usually an event, but it can be anything that shakes up their world. That last bit is essential. The protagonist starts your novel in one state and is forced out of it. Everything changes.

Second, this sudden change forces the character into the action of the story. From the moment that big change occurs, the MC is hurtling towards the climax, when the main conflict will be resolved.

Structurally speaking, the inciting incident generally occurs at the end of the first act of the story (in a traditional three-act approach). The first act establishes our main character and their world, and then we have rising action as the protagonist moves unwittingly toward the inciting incident. When we open the second act, they're dealing with the conflict.

I've seen authors claim their inciting incident happens midway through Act III. I've had authors tell me there are actually two inciting incidents in their book. Some list an inciting incident for each character in the cast, including the antagonist.

None of these is right, y'all. Your novel has one inciting incident. It happens early on. And it drives the protagonist out of their initial emotional state and into the action of the narrative.

Why is it so important to know what your inciting incident is? Because we need it in the blurb. Remember, I explained above that we need drama in the book description. The inciting incident provides that drama because it forces our complacent MC into action. Aside from the climax, it's the most important event in your novel, so we need it to sell the book.

Here are a few examples of inciting incidents you may recognize:

> *"Help me, Obi-Wan Kenobi. You're my only hope."*

> *"Of all the gin joints in all the world, why did she have to walk into mine?"*

> *"You know, you are without a doubt the most interesting single-serving friend I've ever met."*

None of these events occurs at the start of their respective films. Prior to them, the screenwriter establishes normal for the main character. Luke Skywalker is desperate for adventure. Rick Blaine is doing well as a completely neutral party in World War II Casablanca. The Narrator can't sleep and feels lost in contemporary life.

But then, Luke stumbles across the message from Princess Leia. At Ilse's request, Sam plays "As Time Goes By," and Rick comes face to face with the woman who broke his heart. The Narrator's apartment explodes, which leads him to call the mysterious Tyler Durden.

You need to know what the inciting incident of your novel is, so you can include it in the blurb. We'll discuss it in greater detail in Part II: Structure. For now, just remember:

The inciting incident is the external event that forces the main character out of their initial emotional state or situation and into the action of the narrative.

. . .

Homework

I promised you homework at the end of each chapter. There wasn't any in the previous one, because what sort of teacher gives homework on the first day of class?

But now we're into it. It's time to start taking our lessons and applying them. Here's your first assignment:

Pick one-five of your favorite novels or films (mix and match, if you like). For each one:

1. Determine who the main character is. For romance you can pick two

2. Name the stakes for the MC

3. Determine the inciting incident and where it happens in the narrative

Once you've identified those three things for your examples, you should have a good idea of what you'll need to include in your blurb. Next, we'll take a deeper dive into the key components of your blurb as we discuss plot vs. emotion.

CHAPTER 4

PLOT VS. EMOTION

So far, we've talked about the essential elements of an effective fiction blurb. As a reminder, they are:

- Brevity
- Smooth Copy
- Dramatic Phrases
- Character-driven
- Stakes
- Point of View and Tense
- The Inciting Incident

Now, we're going to drill down a little deeper into the real essence of a great book description. To do that, we're going to isolate two of those key ingredients – brevity and character-driven.

To begin, I'm unleashing another of those mind-blowing statements. This one is so big, it's got a whole section of the chapter dedicated to it. Ready? Here we go.

The Plot Doesn't Matter

You read that header right. I'll repeat it, so you can start internalizing. The plot of your novel *does not matter*.

Now, if you're an English major, like I was, you're probably in outright rebellion at the moment. "*Of course*, the plot matters!" you rage. "If you don't have a plot, all you have is a series of vignettes that don't mean anything. That's not literature."

And you are correct ... about what plot is. But that doesn't make it important to a book blurb. Why? Let's remember that the purpose of a description is to *sell* your book, not *summarize* it. And when it comes to selling, the plot gets in our way.

You may still be protesting. "No way, Phoebe," you might be saying. "I have spent the best years of my life developing this carefully crafted story. I tinkered and massaged until every detail was exactly right. Readers appreciate that. If I don't tell them about the plot and how good it is, they won't want to buy."

I get this sentiment. I'm an author myself, and I know all the work that goes into penning a well-plotted story. But believe me when I tell you this: Readers don't care.

Think about it. How many times have you read a book or seen a movie that everyone is raving about, and you just don't get the hype? The research is weak, there are plot holes you could comfortably drive an aircraft carrier through, and the premise isn't even good. How can this be?

You may think it's because readers/viewers have poor taste, the publisher/studio threw a ton of marketing dollars behind it, or some people just get lucky. Well, to quote Val from *A Chorus Line* in her eponymous song, "Dance 10, Looks 3," that ain't it, kid. All of those things may be true, but it isn't what makes a book or film resonate with audiences.

What they care about are *characters*.

Think about the books and films you really treasure. The ones that made a difference to you somehow. Maybe the one that made you want to become an author.

If you're being honest with yourself, it was not the plot that drew you to those books. It was the main character. Even if this is a book you were forced to read for a class in school, the reason it stayed with you is because you identified with the protagonist. Their struggle was relatable. Their solution inspired you. Their world felt familiar.

That is the thing readers remember. It's what makes them reread or rewatch their favorites multiple times.

I'll give you an example of what I mean. *Star Trek II: The Wrath of Khan* is one of my all-time favorite films. The plot is a fairly straightforward action-adventure yarn. Admiral Jim Kirk is leading a training voyage of young Star Fleet cadets aboard his old ship, the *U.S.S. Enterprise*. He's feeling maudlin, because he used to be the captain, making decisions out in the deep reaches of space that affected the lives of entire planetary populations. But now, he's pretty much flying a desk.

However, Kirk's old enemy, Khan, seizes a Federation starship, and uses it to find Kirk, and exact his revenge. There is also a McGuffin of an experimental terraforming project that can be perverted into an Armageddon weapon, and of course, Kirk has access to it and Khan wants it.

Kirk is overmatched due to Khan's genetically engineered superior intellect and the fact that the aging admiral only has trainees aboard the *Enterprise*. On top of that, Khan's first attack is an ambush that disables most of the ship. The climax of the movie sees the two foes circling each other in a nebula that renders sensors blind and shields inoperative, both seeking to get lucky enough to hit their opponent with a photon torpedo for the kill.

It's a taut submarine thriller set in outer space that proceeds at breakneck pace, keeping the viewer breathless until its emotional end. As action films go, it's the gold standard.

This is not why I love it.

Star Trek II is not about Khan's revenge or starship duels. It's not about an apocalyptic weapon falling into the wrong hands. Those things are all part of the movie, but they are the trappings of the plot, not what the film is about.

Rather, it is the story of Jim Kirk and his sense of purposelessness. He opens the film dressing down a cadet for her failure in an exercise in which there is no way to win. His close friend, "Bones" McCoy, calls him out, saying, "Damn it, Jim, what's the matter with you? Other people have birthdays. Why are we treating yours like a funeral?" Later on, his longtime closest counsel and first officer, Spock, says, "If I may be so bold, it was a mistake for you to accept promotion."

Kirk is unhappy in his new job. He's no longer doing what Spock calls his "first, best destiny": commanding a starship. And in the film's dark night of the soul, Kirk himself tells former lover, Carol Marcus, "How do I feel? Old. Worn out."

This is a movie about a man who has lost an essential piece of himself. He finds it when a madman from his past returns for revenge and the son he never knew forgives him. *Star Trek II: The Wrath of Khan* is about death and rebirth. It's about a man coming to terms with his sins and finding a new way forward.

That is why I love it. *Star Trek II* is the film that taught me you can infuse deep human themes into genre fiction. I learned that there is more to writing a satisfying novel than making sure the plot is exciting. I've lost track of how many times I've watched that movie, and I can quote nearly every line in it. And that's because Jim Kirk's emotional journey resonates with me.

This is what you want to give readers in your blurb. Forget the plot. Show them why they will love to root for your main character.

Brevity, Character, and Emotion

So, if the plot doesn't matter, and we need to give them the protagonist, what does that mean for our blurb? Let's go back to those essential elements.

Remember, our book description needs to be brief. We've only got about 200-250 words to work with, and that puts space at a premium. There isn't room for backstory or too much plot. If I were penning a blurb for *Star Trek II*, I wouldn't be able to explain who Khan is, why he hates Kirk, and the subplot of Project: Genesis. I'll lose the reader before I even get to the inciting incident.

I need to focus on my protagonist. We want our blurb to be character-driven. Kirk needs to be the subject of every single sentence. Moreover, each sentence needs to be about his emotional journey through the early parts of the film.

This is where emotion is important to the blurb. Forget the plot. Tell us what your MC is feeling. Tell us why. Give the reader someone they can immediately identify with.

The inciting incident of the book forces your character out of their current state and into the action of the narrative. To do that, we need to know what that emotional situation is. For *Star Trek II*, I'd want to open with how Admiral Kirk is feeling old and that his best days are behind him. That is a familiar feeling to a lot of readers. Whether you're an aging jock dreaming of the glory days of high school or a career woman who feels she never got her opportunity, you may be able to relate to a man who feels like there is nothing more for him to do, even though he still has a lot of life left.

My Best Page Forward colleague, Robert Scanlon, calls this "attaching the reader to your main character." We want to immediately give them someone who looks a little like them in some way. Sure, none of us knows what it's like to battle the Klingons in the far reaches of space, but we can imagine feeling like we no longer matter.

Whatever your protagonist's problem is at the beginning of the book, readers need to know about it. Because the inciting incident is going to come along and change everything, and the resulting conflict is what's going to get them turning pages.

Readers don't identify with plots. They identify with characters. So give them that in your blurb.

Emotional Journey

Just as potential buyers want to know who your protagonist is from an emotional standpoint, they also want to know that character is going to change. If you've taken even one course on novel writing, you've surely been taught that the essence of fiction is conflict. And there's no conflict like personal conflict.

Your main character surely struggles throughout your book. We want to see some of this in the description. So, we start with the MC's initial emotional state. Then, we shake things up with the inciting incident. And *then*, we show how they react.

Once again, the plot doesn't matter. Stay focused on your main character's emotional journey. Keep them as the subject of the sentence. Remain inside their head, not outside looking down.

It doesn't matter that, after the initial encounter with Khan, Kirk retreats *Enterprise* behind Regula-1 to make repairs and then beams to the space station where Genesis is being held. Those are just plot details.

The important part is that he has to come to grips with the fact that he cost the lives of barely trained crewmembers. He made a mistake against Khan, and people died. Because his underestimation of his opponent was so grievous, everyone's life is at risk. In short, he's feeling old because he made a stupid mistake and people are dead as a result.

Kirk's wrestling with his guilt and his personal fear that he really is washed up are what drive him. He's trying to avoid those emotions, so he can focus on fixing the problem. But he can't, and he's forced to face them head-on when he meets his son.

What's interesting about him at this point is not his tactical attempts to deal with an enemy or the mystery of what happened to the Genesis Project. He's compelling because his emotions and his shortcomings threaten to overwhelm him and cost billions of lives.

Will he face his demons in time to defeat a madman? Or will he allow his self-loathing to consume him and everyone he loves? *That* is a conflict that makes readers want to know what happens!

Use Plot to Reveal Emotion

Okay, we've talked a lot about how the plot of your story doesn't matter. But that doesn't mean it isn't a useful tool. After all, you can't really discuss a novel without mentioning *some* of the story elements.

At Best Page Forward, we do this by using the plot to reveal emotion. Except for the opening line of the blurb, every one of our sentences has two clauses – a transition phrase and the main action of the sentence. The transition phrase includes essential plot information necessary to advance the story. And the second clause gives us the emotion. Here's an example of how it works:

> *No longer galloping across the cosmos since accepting promotion to admiral, the Star Fleet hero feels lost for the first time in his illustrious career.*

Let's break this down piece by piece. We can see plot information in the transition phrase. Kirk is "no longer galloping across the cosmos" and he "accepted promotion to admiral." Those are plot points. They're background information that tell the reader important things about our dour MC.

The second part of the sentence shows us Kirk's emotions. He "feels lost for the first time." That's big. You've got a Star Fleet admiral who *feels* lost. This guy is in charge of thousands of lives, and he doesn't know where he's going himself.

I also used that emotional reveal to slip in a little more plot information in service to painting a picture of Kirk's state of mind at the start of the film. Notice how instead of using the pronoun "he," I instead described Kirk as "the Star Fleet hero." Admittedly, "hero" is a loaded term. But this is no ordinary flag officer. He's accomplished, heroic – a fact I emphasized by describing his career as "illustrious."

Notice how Kirk is the subject of the sentence. We see him feeling. He's at the center of this reveal.

We get a whole lot of information about Jim Kirk's emotional state from that single sentence. What we didn't do was tell the reader what was happening in the plot. We used the background information to reveal who our MC is at the beginning of the story.

We'll discuss this tactic in greater depth in Part II: Structure. For now, the thing to bear in mind is that the plot doesn't matter. It's a tool we use to elucidate the protagonist's emotional journey.

Homework

Go back to those one-five movies or books you chose for the last exercise. For each one, identify the main character's emotional journey through the story. Figure out what the story is really about.

Then, write one sentence for each film/novel. Write a transition phrase that gives background or plot information from the story and a main clause that reveals the main character's emotional state or journey.

When you're done, you'll be ready for the next critical piece of a fantastic fiction blurb – agency. Join me in the next chapter to see what I mean.

CHAPTER 5
AGENCY

You've probably heard tons of proverbs about how you are in control of your own destiny. You can choose to be happy. You control your reactions to what other people say. You are the sum of the decisions you make.

Specious platitudes aside, what these ideas all boil down to is having agency in your life. And just as sentimentalists want you to believe that you have agency, your readers want to know that your main character has it, too.

What It Is

Okay, so what am I talking about? When a character has agency, they are the person who is acting. They are in control of what's happening, even if the story is working against them.

When James Bond is tied down to a table with a laser beam creeping slowly towards him, he doesn't have agency. (Weird for a secret *agent*, right?) The agency in this case belongs with the person controlling the laser – Auric Goldfinger.

But Bond takes over the agency in the scene when he claims to know all about Operation: Grand Slam. At that moment, Goldfinger can't be sure what 007 knows and what he doesn't. He isn't certain Bond is lying when he says he's already told his superiors. At that point in the story, Goldfinger can't risk his master plan being spoiled. So, he has to release 007 from his deathtrap to question him further.

In that way, Bond is in charge of what happens. He tricks Goldfinger into turning off the laser.

Agency rests with the person who has control of the situation. And it doesn't have to be external control.

If Lois Lane *thinks* she is a better reporter than Clark Kent, she has agency. It doesn't matter whether she is better or not. Thinking is active, and in the context of that sentence, it gives her agency.

Why It's Important

You might be wondering what the big deal is. After all, putting 007 in a deathtrap is not only a required trope if you're penning a Bond film, it makes for good drama. How *will* our hero escape certain doom?

In Chapter 3, I said we'd be spending a lot of time discussing character, and this is one of those critical – often grossly underestimated – pieces of getting a blurb right. Characters having agency is crucial.

Reading is a form of wish fulfillment. The reason we connect with fictional characters is they confront their issues and come away better for it. They face down evil and conquer it. An entire generation of children fell in love with Harry Potter, because he (and Ron and Hermione) were so easy to identify with. Plus, Harry and the gang always won. That feels pretty great if you're a thirteen-year-old (or even a 113-year-old) who feels disempowered by parents, bullies, teachers, or just your own awkwardness.

No matter what sort of fiction you like to read, the pleasure in it comes from imagining yourself alongside the hero, making the decisions that win the day. And the reason that's so intoxicating is that we rarely get the same opportunities in our own lives. Whether we're struggling to pass trigonometry or terrified of giving a presentation to the boss, we're stuck in a mundane, ordinary world where there are no dragons to slay and rotten people only seem to get rewarded instead of the comeuppance they so richly deserve.

It's a fact that most of us don't have agency in our own lives the way we'd like. That doesn't mean we're powerless and that we don't have some control over our destinies. But we don't have the same ability to conquer our foes that our literary heroes do.

In short, our favorite characters fight – and win – battles that we cannot.

Selling is all about understanding the buyer. You need to know what they desire, so that you can explain to them how you offer it. Readers of fiction want protagonists they can relate to, that they can root for.

And it's no fun rooting for someone who is knocked around by life and never seems to get any control over what's happening to them.

When you are crafting your blurb, you can subtly and powerfully hint to the reader that your MC is going to deliver the kind of satisfying victory they crave. All you have to do is give your protagonist agency in every single sentence.

How to Give It

Ensuring a character has agency is simpler than you might think. Remember back in Chapter 4, when I discussed Jim Kirk being the subject of the sentence? That is the prerequisite for giving him agency. Likewise, in our example above, *Lois Lane thinks she's a better reporter than Clark Kent*, "Lois Lane" is the subject of the sentence, and "thinks" is the predicate. That sets her up to have agency.

But there is a little catch here. Not just any verb will do. To really lock that agency in, you need strong, active verbs. We're talking words like:

- Struggles

- Grapples
- Battles
- Embraces
- Masters
- Confronts
- Attacks

That's not nearly an exhaustive list. But see how each one of them implies action? Notice too how each has strong emotion attached to it. Emotive, active, powerful verbs really drive your hero forward and help give them agency in the sentence.

Now, you *can* use forms of the verb "to be," and still have an agented character. For example, we could write:

> *Lois Lane is desperate to prove she's a better reporter than Clark Kent.*

Lois is still the subject of the sentence, and "is" gives her a degree of agency, because it describes how she is feeling. She's desperate. But that is a much weaker verb than an active one.

(For those of you wondering about "prove," it may be a strong verb, but it's not the predicate of the sentence. It's part of an objective prepositional phrase that modifies "desperate," not "Lois Lane" or "is." See? Told you I had to diagram sentences when I was in school.)

Sometimes, you just have to use a form of the verb "to be." It's not a terrible choice. But wherever possible, go for an active, powerful verb. It makes the agency stronger, and the sentence more dynamic.

Must Not Use "Must"

There's another little trick we need to call out when it comes to agenting your protagonist. That is the use of the word, "must," and its variations – "forced to," "have to," "has to," etc. "Must" is a sinister, little word that shows up a lot in book descriptions. Here's an example:

> *To save her family, Gina must conquer her inner demons and learn to live without the bottle.*

On the surface that reads powerfully. We've got Gina wrestling with her inner demons and trying to quit drinking. Her family is at risk. Those are pretty high stakes. We've got a ton of drama here. There's just one problem:

Gina doesn't have any agency.

You may be thinking, "What are you talking about, Phoebe? She's the subject of the sentence, and 'conquer' is a strong, powerful verb!" These things are true.

But unfortunately, "must" came in and ruined the whole thing.

My colleague at Best Page Forward, Jim Heskett, calls "must" an agency thief. Here's why. When a character "must" do something, they have no choice. They have no self-determination. They are being acted upon by the universe or some other external force instead of *choosing* to take action. As soon as something is acting upon them, they are no longer in control.

Think back to when you were in middle or high school. You were planning to go to a movie with your friends. Your mom tells you that you're not going unless you clean your room first. So, to go to the movie, you *must* clean your room.

You just lost all your agency.

Now, you could choose *not* to do what Mom said. But then you're not going out with friends. There is a choice here, but it's no choice at all. Mom has all the power. She has the agency. You're stuck with having to do something you don't want to if you want to go out.

To give Gina some agency, we need to cut "must" out of that sentence. What if we tried this:

> *With her family at stake, Gina realizes she it's time to conquer her inner demons and learn to live without the bottle.*

Bam! We just put Gina in control of the situation. She *realizes* it's time. That is an active sentence with her as the subject. Here's another way to do it:

> *Now, Gina faces a terrible choice: Live without the bottle or lose her family forever.*

This isn't the strongest sentence in terms of strong, active verbs. But, Gina *faces* the choice. She has some agency here, and that's important. She's not forced to choose between her family and alcohol. She is facing that choice. It's a subtle difference in word choice, but it's everything in terms of making the character more appealing.

Remember, readers want to revel in the conquests of their heroes. They dive into your fiction because they crave the wish fulfillment you provide. No one wishes to be forced to do anything. So, give your readers what they want – an agented MC they can root for.

Homework

Go back to the one-five films/books you chose in Chapter 3. Pick an important scene from each one that you think you would include if you were writing a blurb. Then, write a sentence for each one describing it, making sure to give the protagonist agency. Remember:

- Make them the subject of the sentence
- Wherever possible, use a dynamic, powerful verb
- Avoid using forms of "must"

Our next lesson should feel familiar to fiction writers everywhere – "show" vs. "tell." Once you've completed your agency homework, turn the page, and we'll get started.

CHAPTER 6

SHOW 'N' TELL

If you've taken even one class on fiction-writing, you've heard the author's Golden Rule: Show; Don't Tell. It's an important principle that applies not just to your novel but also to the blurb used to sell it. Let's take a quick moment to unpack it before diving into specifically how to apply it to copywriting.

When you describe action, you can do it one of two ways: You can *tell* the reader what happens, or you can *show* it happening. Here are a few examples:

> **Tell:** *Andy's birthday is never a big deal to Woody. After all, he's Andy's favorite toy and has been for forever.*
>
> **Show:** *Woody knows he has nothing to fear on Andy's birthday. As the undisputed favorite toy since forever, he can't imagine anything in those packages would threaten the special place in his boy's heart.*

Let's look at the first version. Woody is the protagonist in *Toy Story*, but in our opening line, he's not even the subject of the sentence. "Andy's birthday" is. So that tells us right away that he has no agency, which is not what we want.

More importantly, though, with the sentence being about the birthday, we're *telling the reader* about the plot instead of letting them know about Woody.

In the second sentence, we double down on this technique. We tell the reader that Woody is Andy's favorite toy. We don't show them. He may be the subject of the sentence this time, but he still doesn't have any real agency. We're simply telling the reader something about him.

By way of contrast, our second example puts Woody firmly at the center of what's happening. Woody knows he has nothing to fear. He can't imagine anything threatening him. Woody is in control. And we're not telling the reader about what is happening to Woody; we're showing his reaction to the upcoming event of Andy's birthday party.

Here's another example:

> **Tell:** *After crash-landing on a strange planet, Buzz Lightyear needs to repair his ship. But none of the native lifeforms have any idea how to help him.*

See how we're telling? We told the reader that Buzz crash-landed, that he needs to repair his ship, and that the natives are unhelpful. What if instead we did it like this?

> **Show:** *Buzz Lightyear feels all alone. Crash-landing on a strange planet with no communication with Star Command, the galaxy's bravest Space Ranger tries in vain to get assistance from the natives to repair his ship.*

In this version, we can see what's happening. We know Buzz feels all alone. We see him try vainly to get help to repair his disabled ship. All the facts are the same. But the way they are presented makes all the difference in the world.

. . .

The Importance of POV

All right, with the basics of show vs. tell nailed down, let's circle back to that all-important concept of character. You'll recall from the previous chapter on agency that readers want characters who can succeed where perhaps they cannot. They are looking for characters they can root for, people they identify with. They want heroes and people who feel like friends. If you happen to write in a genre like vigilante justice or grimdark fantasy that generally features antiheroes, readers are looking for someone who can do what they themselves cannot.

Whether your audience is looking for empowerment or familiarity, it is the characters they want to know about. Remember, the plot doesn't matter. Characters do.

With that in mind, let's have another look at the first example from *Toy Story*:

> *Andy's birthday is never a big deal to Woody. After all, he's Andy's favorite toy and has been for forever.*

We've already discussed how this version is telling the reader about the plot instead of showing them anything about Woody. It's pretty easy to spot why this is: We're not inside Woody's point of view. If you look at those sentences carefully, you can see that we're outside of his perspective.

I call this the thousand-foot view of the character. We're way up above Woody, looking down on his life. *Andy's birthday is never a big deal to Woody.* As I mentioned above, Woody isn't even the subject of the sentence. That's tell.

Likewise, *he's Andy's favorite toy*. Again, we're looking down on Woody here. We're telling the reader an important fact – Woody is Andy's favorite toy. But we're not showing them.

Think about the opening credit sequence of *Toy Story*. We see Andy playing with Woody. He clearly is the central figure of the action. He rescues Bo Peep from Mr. Potato Head. He gets placed in a special spot on the bed when Andy is called downstairs. The writers of *Toy Story* understood that to set Woody up for the main conflict of the story, it was much more powerful to *show* him as the favorite toy instead of telling us. That way, when Mr. Potato Head says Woody is the favorite at the staff meeting, it resonates.

Showing is always more powerful than telling. We therefore want to do it in our blurb, too.

That's why POV is so important. When we are looking out through the MC's eyes, we're seeing the world they inhabit rather than being told about it. Let's look at the second version of that example now:

> *Woody knows he has nothing to fear on Andy's birthday. As the undisputed favorite toy since forever, he can't imagine anything in those packages would threaten the special place in his boy's heart.*

The opening two words put us directly in Woody's head. "Woody knows." And then we find out more – "he has nothing to fear ..." We've immediately established our protagonist as confident, self-assured. And we didn't tell the reader, "Woody is confident." Instead, we showed them – "Woody knows he has nothing to fear on Andy's birthday."

In the second sentence we learn more about why he is so comfortable with his position: "As the undisputed favorite toy since forever ..."

"Wait a minute, Phoebs!" I hear you thinking. "Woody's not the subject there. That's something that's outside his head."

Let's roll back to Chapter 4. Remember how we talked about using plot to reveal emotion? Well, that's a plot phrase there – "As the undisputed favorite toy since forever ..." That's all background information, but it's in the transition phrase. Let's look at the main body of the sentence:

> *... he can't imagine anything in those packages would threaten the special place in his boy's heart.*

See how we're right back in Woody's perspective? "... he couldn't imagine ..." That's Woody's thought process. Nothing in any of those boxes is going to come between Woody and his boy. We're seeing the entire setup from Woody's perspective. Not only does he have agency in the sentence, we're inside his head, looking out at the world.

That forms a connection with the reader. Everyone on Earth has at some point felt the sensation of being replaced. Everyone has felt totally betrayed. And it's usually a surprise.

Readers can feel it coming, though. They're thinking, "Oh, no, Woody! Something's going to happen to you! Somehow, this birthday is going to be different!"

The anticipation of the inciting incident has sucked the reader in. They are living Woody's life now. This wonderful, happy toy is about to have his whole existence turned upside down. Not only can we feel it coming; we're already sympathetic to the totally unaware MC.

And that setup makes the inciting incident land so hard. Woody isn't just replaced. His replacement doesn't realize he is a toy and doesn't feel the same responsibility towards the others that Woody does. It's infuriating! Especially when the *other toys* seem to think Buzz Lightyear is cooler, too.

None of that would hit with nearly the same impact if we just told the reader what is happening. By letting them experience it through Woody, they're a lot more invested in the outcome. That makes them want to know what happens next.

So, don't look down on your protagonist from way up high. Zoom in and look out at the world through their eyes.

Emotion Words

Being inside the MC's head helps us see the world as they do. But what we really want is to get the reader experiencing the story with the character. We want them on that same freight train of feelings. When they're sharing the emotional experience, it deepens the connection with the protag and further encourages them to want to know more.

Once again, word choice goes a long way toward making this happen. Verbs in particular can really help out here. Remember how we want to focus on action verbs instead of forms of the "to be" verb? Well, not only do those more dynamic words help give agency, they can also ramp up the emotional content. Here are a few examples:

- Fears
- Vows
- Yearns
- Desires
- Laments
- Agonizes
- Devastates

Once again, that's not nearly an exhaustive list. But notice how each of those words is full of emotion. We feel something when we read those words. If I'm upset, that's one level of emotion. But if I'm devastated, that's a whole order of magnitude larger. Choosing strong, emotive verbs really drives your character's feelings into the reader's heart.

They can also dress up forms of "to be." Sometimes, we can't really avoid saying a character is something or another. But if we add a powerful, emotion verb to it, the stakes go up. For example, I could write:

> *Joe is sad that things didn't work out.*

That would give us a sense of Joe's emotional state. But "is" as a form of "to be" is kind of weak. On the other hand, I could make a compound verb by attaching one of those big-emotion words and have something like this:

> *Joe is devastated when things don't work out.*

Suddenly, the stakes have gone way up. Not only is "devastated" stronger than "sad," but notice how, by conveying the emotion in the verb instead of as part of an objective phrase, it lands with much greater impact.

We can also use emotion verbs in our transition phrases. Staying with "devastated" we could do something like:

> *Devastated when things don't work out, Joe refuses to even consider risking his heart again.*

Now, we've got a ton of emotion in the transition – which we've used to sneak in our plot information – before we move onto the action of the sentence.

In addition to verbs, you can inject emotion into a sentence with adjectives and adverbs and gerunds. Saying someone has a "gloomy disposition," or is "deliriously happy," or that "grieving takes its toll," all use powerful words to increase the emotional value of a sentence or phrase. Doing that raises a reader's interest in the MC's conflict and journey.

Homework

Take a look at those one-five books or movies you chose one more time. Ask yourself, "What is the main character's emotional journey?" Forget the plots for a moment. What emotions are the protagonists experiencing or struggling with?

Now, write two sentences for each novel or film. In both of them, focus on writing from inside the character's perspective. Look out through their eyes at the world instead of down on them from above.

Use emotionally charged words, especially verbs, to describe this person's journey. Let the reader see what they are feeling.

We have one more subject to cover in blurb theory. We're going to consider what exactly we should put in, content-wise. Finish your homework, then let's find out!

CHAPTER 7

CONTENT AND LANGUAGE CONCERNS

What goes into your blurb and how you express it make a lot of difference towards getting the sale. We've already discussed the importance of emotion words. Here, we're going to look at some important basics about manipulating the language for the most engaging results.

What to Include

First, let's briefly have a look at what you'll need to have in your book description. There are a lot of fallacies and bad advice circulating around the InterWebz about what a blurb should do, what it should have in it, and what it shouldn't. Let's examine what you actually need, debunking myths as we go.

How much of the story do I include?

The short answer to this question is, "As much as it takes to sell the book." There is no hard-and-fast limit.

I frequently encounter authors who say things like, "I was told the blurb should only cover the first fifty pages of the novel." I understand the sentiment behind this fallacy: You don't want to give too much away, or people won't need to buy the book.

There are so many reasons why this is wrong. First, let's look at the practical ones. Let's say you've written a seventy-five-page novella. If you follow the fifty-pages rule, you have to describe two-thirds of the book. That seems like it might spoil a few things.

Let's assume you've written a thousand-page epic. Limit yourself to fifty pages, and you've described what? The first scene? Maybe the second?

Placing an arbitrary limit on how much of the book you describe is foolish. Give yourself as much room as you need to get the reader hooked.

Second, and more importantly, this worry about spoiling misses the point of a blurb. Let's go back to Chapter 2. What is a description's purpose? To *sell* the book, not summarize it.

Look, I'm sure your plot is intricately crafted and well-written. But readers don't care about the plot at this point. They've read all the plots there are. You have your own unique take on things, but your plot is not original. Like every other story out there, it's been done before. Multiple times.

And that's perfectly okay. Human beings like repetition. We like familiar things. We enjoy seeing something we know executed well.

Your book description's job is to sell your novel. And to do that, it needs to focus on the main character's emotional journey.

By now, all this should be review. We've gone over these principles in previous chapters. But they bear repeating here, so you don't limit yourself. Focus on the character's emotional journey, not how much of the plot to give away.

What about spoilers?

A big swerve the reader doesn't expect is a tried-and-true storytelling technique. Whether it's the true identity of Kaiser Sozé, the answer to what's in the box, or The Old Man having bought that Red Ryder

Range Model Air Rifle and hidden it behind the desk, the Big Reveal is always a crowd-pleaser. So, you wouldn't want to include it in the blurb, right?

Well, *probably* not. If it happens towards the end of the book, that's definitely spoiler territory. If it's closer to the beginning, though, it ain't as big a secret as you might think.

Revealing that Darth Vader is Luke Skywalker's father would be a big no-no in the blurb for *The Empire Strikes Back*. That swerve happens at the film's climax.

But *confirming* he's Luke's father in the blurb for *Return of the Jedi* is not a spoiler. Why? Because Yoda admits it early in the movie's second act.

Moreover, it's absolutely critical to the rest of the story's action. Forget all the stuff that goes down on Endor with the Ewoks and the power station. Luke Skywalker is the main character of the original *Star Wars* trilogy. As the third act in the epic, *Return of the Jedi* forces Luke into the final confrontation with his father. Luke's desperate attempt to redeem Darth Vader rather than destroy him is the crux of the film. It is that redemption that ultimately defeats the emperor and saves the Rebellion.

We can't write an accurate and effective blurb for *Return of the Jedi* without discussing Luke facing his father with the destiny of the entire galaxy at stake.

At Best Page Forward, we ask authors to give us a four-act summary of their novels. We ask them to name anything that might be a spoiler, so we don't include it. But for the most part, anything that happens in the first two acts is fair game. It's in the front half of the book, and it is likely important to the emotional journey of the main character. If an author tells us something in the first act is a spoiler, we reach out and try to explain that it isn't.

Here's an unpleasant newsflash: Reviewers don't worry about spoilers. When people review your book on Amazon (which is something you want them to do), they happily tell other readers what happens. *Most* reviewers don't spoil endings or other huge swerves. But if it happens in the first half of the novel, you can count on a reviewer mentioning it.

You have to tell people some of what happens in your novel. (I'm lookin' at you, mystery writers.) You need to attach them to your main character. And whether you like it or not, that includes spoiling some of the story.

How many characters can I have?

This is another question with a layered answer. The short, simple reply is: "One. Two if it's a romance."

But obviously, unless you're writing a blurb for *Castaway* or some other story where there is pretty much *only* one character, there are other people orbiting around the MC. So how many do you include?

If we go back to Chapter 2, you'll recall that we need to keep things brief, that the human mind can really only keep two, maybe three, new ideas straight at once. We can't overburden the reader with too many characters, or they'll get confused. Why? The confused mind says no.

So, name your protagonist. Skip all other names. Refer to those other people according to their relationship to the MC – "her boyfriend," "his brother," "their boss," etc. This does two really important things. First, it keeps it simple for the reader. They don't have to remember that Sylvia is Frank's wife, when they come across her name. They can just refer to her as his wife, spouse, partner, etc.

Second, it keeps that focus squarely on the protagonist. Everyone else's identity revolves around the MC. That puts them at the center of the action and helps us see out through their eyes.

Language

I've already discussed at length how manipulating language is a key aspect of writing effective ad copy. Here, we'll dive into a couple of dos and don'ts.

Power Words

We've discussed this several times already. Stronger, more evocative words sell better. Remember, we've only got about 200 to 250 words to make that sale. We need language that really delivers a punch.

Once again, verbs are your friend here. Wherever possible, go for the strongest version of a verb you can find. For example, "yearns" is much more powerful than "wants." "Smacks" is stronger than "hits." "Dispatches" is more evocative than "kills."

We want to use words that paint a picture. Remember when I said copywriting is more like poetry than prose? This is one of the ways we make that happen. We can say so much more by writing, "John Bender despises rules," than we can with, "John Bender doesn't like rules." Finding rules despicable is a lot more powerful than not liking them.

Look for opportunities to get those power words in. They're shortcuts that let you say so much. With limited space to work with, they are excellent tools for raising stakes and emotion.

Naughty Words

You need to keep your audience in mind when you're selecting what sorts of words to use in your blurb. It used to be that swearing in a book description was a big no-no. But the world has changed. For good or ill, we live in a coarser society than our parents did.

However, so-called naughty words still read stronger on the page than they sound to your ears. I suspect this has to do with becoming desensitized to our environments. If your co-workers are constantly cussing, those words don't hold the same impact as they would if you were, say, in church. We don't expect to *see* them, though, in a news story, a PowerPoint presentation, or a book description. That makes them land a lot harder.

You have to know what your audience is looking for. If you write clean-and-wholesome romance or middle-grade fiction, a word as tame as "hell" is going to sink sales. Those readers (or in the case of MG, parents) do not want to read naughty words. They are looking for G-rated fiction, and if you give any hint that you're crossing into PG territory, they will not buy.

On the other hand, if you write snarky urban fantasy or erotic romance, readers will expect stronger language. In those cases, it may be okay to drop in some words you didn't used to be able to say on television. It's okay to describe your MC as a "badass" or the billionaire maverick as "hotter-than-Hell." That gives readers a clue about what they will discover inside.

But you still want to keep things PG. S-words and F-bombs are too strong for effective ad copy, and they are often in violation of Amazon's own creative acceptance policies. They're perfectly fine in your narrative, where you should use whatever language is appropriate for your audience and story. But when it comes to selling the book, keep the swearing out of it.

Finishing Strong

Speaking of power words, every sentence should end with a bang. As with all things, we remember best what we last saw or heard. So, you want the big idea of each sentence to be at the end. Just as a boxer jabs several times before following with a hook punch or an uppercut, you want the power of each sentence to steadily rise.

For example, in *Bull Durham*, Crash Davis is attracted to Annie Savoy the moment he lays eyes on her. But before he can really make a move, Nuke steps in and immediately (and like all things with Nuke, unwittingly) creates a love triangle.

This is the inciting incident of the movie, and as a result it would have to be in our blurb. Crash wants Annie. But when Nuke arrives, she expresses interest in the young pitcher – a guy who is at least a decade younger than she. And that inflames Crash's jealousy, even though they've just met.

When we structure this sentence in the blurb, we want to get the biggest idea at the end. It may be the greatest baseball movie ever made, but *Bull Durham* is a romantic comedy. So, the Crash-Annie sexual tension has to be front and center in the blurb. Consider this:

> *But when the kid he's supposed to "mature" comes on to the most intriguing woman he's ever met, the grizzled catcher refuses to back down.*

That's a pretty good start. We've got Nuke interfering with Crash's mojo, and Crash puffing up his chest and not letting the kid move in on the girl he's interested in.

But we're a little vague here. What exactly does, "refuses to back down" mean? And what's it got to do with Nuke coming on to Annie? What if we made a slight change:

> *But when the kid he's supposed to "mature" comes on to the most intriguing woman he's ever met, the grizzled catcher is surprised when feelings of jealousy he's never had before surface.*

Now, we're getting somewhere. We've clarified the big idea. Crash is jealous and he doesn't know why. He's meeting both Annie and Nuke for the first time. While he's predisposed to hate Nuke due to the circumstances of Crash's arrival in Durham, he doesn't understand why he should care about this older woman being attracted to a twenty-something kid.

However, "surface" is an active verb, which is good, but it doesn't really give Crash a lot of agency. It's also not the biggest idea in the sentence. The big idea is Crash's jealousy. So, let's rework this one more time:

> *But when the kid he's supposed to "mature" comes on to the most intriguing woman he's ever met, the grizzled catcher is stunned by unfamiliar feelings of jealousy.*

Now, we've got the biggest idea at the end. Crash is jealous. That's what the reader is going to remember.

Homework

By now, you should have several sample blurb sentences from your chosen movies/books. Pick out a few of them and practice editing. Make sure:

- They are in third-person present tense
- Check to see if the MC has agency
- Are we inside the protagonist's head looking out?
- Ensure that the strongest idea is at the end

This concludes all the lessons on blurb theory. By now, you should have a good understanding of the elements of a successful book description. In the next section, we're going to get into the practical. We'll examine the exact structure your blurb should take and go sentence-by-sentence, so you know what to put where and why.

Ready? Let's get started!

CHAPTER 8

THE BASIC STRUCTURE OF A FICTION BLURB

Woo-hoo! We've made it through all the prerequisites. We now have a strong command of blurb theory. It's time to put that knowledge into practical use.

At Best Page Forward, we've spent years developing our formula. The more we learned about what was actually working, the more we tweaked it. At the time of this writing, the rubric you're about to see was six years in the making and has proven highly effective, regardless of genre. Obviously, it works a little differently for, say, horror than children's picture books. But the basic principles are the same, regardless of what you're writing.

There are two templates for fiction blurbs and a third one for memoirs, which we'll discuss in Chapter 19. All three are collected in Appendix A for easy reference.

Terminology

A few terms you'll want to keep in mind, so that things will make sense. At Best Page Forward, we divide a book description into four distinct parts. These are:

- The Hook/Headline
- The Body/Synopsis
- The Selling Paragraph
- The Call to Action

The body/synopsis is the biggest chunk (as you might imagine), and it is the only one that is comprised of more than one paragraph. For our purposes here, I'm going to break the entire blurb down into individual sentences. When I'm discussing the body, I'll use some abbreviations.

"P" stands for "paragraph." "S" is for "sentence." And a number indicates where it goes in the sequence. For example, "P1S3" would be short for "Paragraph 1, Sentence 3." Make sense?

Great! Without further ado, here it comes: The Best Page Forward formula for fiction blurbs!

Standard Fiction Blurb Template

Most book descriptions walk this path. They follow the early emotional journey of a single main character in this exact fashion:

The Hook

P1S1: *The Gut Punch*

P1S2: *The Expansion*

P1S3: *The Inciting Incident*

P2S1: *The Bridge*

P2S2: *The Complication*

The Cliffhanger

The Selling Paragraph

The Call to Action (CTA)

Wow, that's a lot of interesting words and phrases. But what do they mean?

We'll fully explore each sentence in its own chapter. (Yes, each one is that important.) For now, here are some quick definitions:

The Hook

Think of this as a newspaper headline. Its job is to grab attention and get the reader interested. If the hook does what it is supposed to, the reader is intrigued, wants to know more, and checks out the first paragraph.

The Gut Punch

This melodramatic term describes your opening sentence. It's when we first introduce the reader to the MC, and it's got a fighting name, because we want it to land with a lot of force.

The Expansion

Our second sentence builds on the foundation we laid in the first. We expand on the raw emotions we laid out in P1S1 and then raise the stakes for the character. Which sets us up for ...

The Inciting Incident

We've discussed what this is back in Part I: Blurb Theory. There are two important things to know here. First, it goes in P1S3. Second, it should always be presented as a cliffhanger. More on that in Chapter 12.

The Bridge

This is the first sentence of our second paragraph. We call it "the bridge" because its job is to get from the end of P1 into our new situation in P2. Think of the paragraph break as a river we need to get our reader across, so they can become further engaged with our MC.

The Complication

At this point, we've established our protagonist, turned their world inside-out with the inciting incident, and then bridged from that causal force to a new emotional state. Now, it's time to put everything into doubt. The complication is something major that could prevent the protag from accomplishing their goal.

The Cliffhanger

At Best Page Forward, we actually call this "The Final Cliffhanger" because P1S3 and P2S2 should both be cliffhanger-y in their structure. I'm shortening it here to keep things simple and clear.

The cliffhanger is always presented as a question, asking whether or not the hero will succeed. It raises the stakes as high as they can possibly go. We'll discuss stakes more in subsequent chapters. For now, know that you need them to be at their absolute zenith by the end of the cliffhanger.

The Selling Paragraph

As the name implies, this is actually two sentences, each of which serves to sell. The first, SPS1, if you will, is called, "What It Is," and succinctly categorizes your book. SPS2 is titled, "Why You Want It," and lists several features of the novel that will encourage readers to buy. We'll discuss both of these in greater detail in Chapter 16.

The Call to Action

Good sales copy always includes a call to action, or "CTA," at the end. Its job, as the name implies, is to tell the audience what you want them to do.

At Best Page Forward we like to make these clever, so they stand out, and we'll discuss that in Chapter 17. For now, the main thing to remember is that the CTA tells the reader what we want them to do. For that reason, it always includes the words, "buy today."

The 2-POV Fiction Blurb Template

If you're a romance author, you know you have to talk about both of the lovers in the story. You essentially have two main characters, who each need equal time.

Some other types of novels benefit from this as well. Literary fiction, women's fiction, and books with parallel narratives sometimes do better with a second POV in the blurb. In those cases, we use the template below:

The Hook

P1S1: *The Gut Punch*

P1S2: *The Expansion*

P1S3: *The Inciting Incident*

P2S1: *The Uppercut*

P2S2: *The Inciting Incident (Again)*

P2S3: *The Consequence*

P3S1: *The First Complication*

P3S2: *The Second Complication*

The Cliffhanger

The Selling Paragraph

The Call to Action

As you can see, the first paragraph of a 2-POV blurb is identical to the standard template. The same is true of the cliffhanger, the selling paragraph, and the call to action.

But P2 is different, and there is a P3, where we didn't have one in the standard template. I'll discuss these differences in much greater detail in Chapter 18. The thing to know now is that P2 is dedicated to our second POV character, and P3 splits time between MC1 and MC2.

Homework

Okay, it's time to start really thinking in terms of writing a blurb. Up until this point, we've practiced specific techniques. Now, we're going to get practical.

Go back to your books/films you've been working on each chapter. For now, treat them as single POV, even if they are romances. Pick out the main character or the most-main character. Then, determine what the content should be for each sentence in the blurb. You don't need to worry about actually writing those out. Just make a note of what you believe needs to be in each sentence. If you get stuck, identify the inciting incident. Put that in P1S3 and work backwards to the start of the story. Likewise, figure out what a major complication is and put that in P2S2. For P2S1, ask yourself what would go between that and the inciting incident.

You may be tempted to start using your own book at this point, but I encourage you to stick with our example novels/movies. The goal here will be to practice really crafting a good blurb and seeing how it's done *before* attacking your own work. All of us are too close to our own creative process to view it objectively. (I struggle to write blurbs as good for my own work as I do for BPF clients.) Practice on someone else's material to make it easier on yourself. You'll feel more confident when it's time to do it for your book.

Over the next several chapters we're going to dive deeply into each sentence in your book description. When you've got your homework completed, we'll get right into our first section – The Hook!

CHAPTER 9
THE HOOK

The hook is arguably the most important part of the blurb. We sometimes refer to it as the headline since it sits at the top of the blurb. Indeed, when we format descriptions for clients, we code the hook to be in H4 (headline level 4 for those who don't know HTML). We want them to be bold and stand out.

A lot of things go into making a great hook. That's why this chapter is one of the longest in the book, because there is a *lot* to think about when crafting great ones. Let's start with some basics first.

Definition

The hook's name is hopefully self-explanatory. Think of it like you're fishing. The blurb is your rod, reel, and line. The headline is your fishhook, done up with a tasty worm or a shiny lure. We cast it out into the water and hope to attract some hungry readers.

When it does its job correctly, it hooks a reader, so you can reel them in with the rest of your blurb. If everything is strong enough, you'll land them in the boat by having them click the Buy button.

Everything rests on setting the hook. If you only master one thing in this book, make it writing great hooks. When a reader is intrigued by your headline, they'll keep reading, getting more and more engaged until they have to know what happens.

But we have to get them reading first, which is the hook's job.

Hooks vs. Taglines

Hooks and taglines sometimes get mixed together. In the same way that "blurb" came to mean "book description," some folks see "hook" and "tagline" as synonymous.

I find it more useful to differentiate. To be sure, they're both short pieces of ad copy designed to sell books (or movies). But in my view, a tagline is *really* short. It may not even be a whole sentence.

The real difference between them is how they work. A tagline invokes emotion. A hook tells us a little something about the story.

I'm sure you're getting ready to remind me that I've said selling books is all about emotion. Don't worry; I'm not contradicting myself. But where a hook raises emotional tension by revealing what the main character wants, what's standing in their way, and what the consequences of failure are, the tagline is only trying to engage your interest by inciting an emotion in you.

Let's look at a few of the more famous taglines in history:

> *In space, no one can hear you scream.*

This incredibly memorable line invokes powerful emotions. It's so good, you probably don't need me to tell you it's from Ridley Scott's 1979 masterpiece, *Alien*. What makes it so good is the visceral sense of fear it creates. We know without question that this is a horror movie. Because if we're screaming and want to be heard, it's probably because we're desperate for someone to come help. And if no one can hear you, well ...

Because the opening clause is, "in space," we know this horror movie is going to take place in outer space. That will increase the fear of isolation, of no one being able to come to the rescue. (And it's one of the things that makes *Alien* work so well.)

But we don't actually know anything about the story from this tagline. If you've not seen the movie, you may not know it's about a monster that horrifically hitched a ride with an unsuspecting ore-hauling crew. We may be in outer space, but what is the tech level? Did this happen on one of the moonshot missions of the Sixties? Is it set in the far future? Who are these people, and why did they encounter the titular alien?

None of that is clear or even hinted at by the tagline. All the tagline says is "scary movie in space."

On the other hand, we could do something like:

> *A desperate crew. An unwelcome passenger. In space, no one can hear you scream.*

Now, we've got a better idea what's happening. We've got this desperate crew that has an unwelcome passenger aboard. The chilling tagline tells us what's at stake. These people are in serious trouble from this unwelcome passenger. And by "serious trouble," I mean, "They're gonna die." *That's* a strong hook.

Here's another one of my favorites:

> *You will believe a man can fly.*

That line beautifully captures the essence of *Superman: The Movie*. When we think of Superman, one of the first things that comes to mind is his ability to "leap tall buildings in a single bound." And one of the things that made Richard Donner's 1978 masterwork so great was the use of blue-screen technology and wire techniques imported from Hong Kong martial arts films that gave us the best look Hollywood had created at that time of a superhero flying across the skyline. All the feelings that *Superman: The Movie* brought to theaters are perfectly encompassed in that tagline.

But it doesn't tell us anything about the story or even the main character. We don't see anything about Clark Kent's humble background, Lois Lane's relentless fire, or Lex Luthor's sinister plan to destroy the West Coast. To do that, we'd need something like:

> *He's the only survivor of a once-great planet. If he can't stop a greedy madman, his new home is doomed.*

That exaggerates the stakes a little bit, since Luthor isn't trying to blow up the whole world, just California. But it gives us an idea of what's going on here. The Last Son of Krypton is in a battle to save his adopted home.

Taglines can be useful. A lot of authors like to put them on their book covers, and that's a good place for them. (Just keep in mind, they'll only be legible on the print copy and on the eBook cover on your actual sales page. In ads, they're going to be too small to read.)

For your blurb, you want to use a hook. It gives the reader a little more to go on, and more importantly, it names the stakes.

Elements

Before you can begin to craft an effective hook, you need to know the answer to three questions:

- *What does the main character want?*
- *What is standing in their way?*
- *What are the consequences of failure?*

Let's quickly review what we learned in the last section. Readers relate to characters, and they want to make an emotional connection with them. The plot doesn't matter, so it's all about the character.

With all that in mind, we really need to know what the MC wants. Are they hoping to get married? Do they need to stop a doomsday device? Are they looking to master their magical powers? Would they just like to be understood?

Whatever is the main driver behind the character's actions over the course of the narrative needs to be in your hook. It's what readers will connect to.

Wanting something isn't enough, though. To have conflict, which you'll recall we established is the essence of fiction, something has to be standing in the protagonist's way. So, what is it?

Does their overbearing mother run off everyone they're interested in? Can that bomb only be defused by someone who reads Hungarian? Is the teacher who can help them with their powers on the other side of a huge sea? Do they have debilitating anxiety that makes it impossible to open up to other people?

There has to be an obstacle. Whatever it is, it should show up in the hook.

Finally, wanting something and having a roadblock in the way are not enough for great fiction. There need to be consequences for *not* getting it. More importantly, those consequences have to matter.

Will our MC lose their inheritance if they don't get married? How many people will die if that doomsday device goes off? What happens if the protagonist *doesn't* actually master those powers? If our tortured main character isn't able to be understood, how will they suffer?

All of this is important. When a reader sees a character in want or need of something important, but there is an obstacle in the way and bad things will happen if they don't get it, their intrigue shoots off the charts. Just like that shiny, fishing lure, the person is attracted, interested, (Dare I say it?), hooked.

So, when you're plotting out that hook, make sure you've got the answer to those three, critical questions not just in your head, but on the page.

. . .

Stakes

What's at stake is another way of asking, "What are the consequences of failure?" What's at stake if the character doesn't get what they want?

But it's bigger than that, too. From the start of your hook, all the way to the end, the stakes need to be steadily rising. They're bigger in the middle than they are at the beginning. And they're bigger still at the end. If your stakes are not steadily increasing, you're treading water, not moving anywhere. And if you move too slowly, you'll lose readers.

We want to start with high stakes at the start of the hook and keep escalating them until the end. As we learned in Part I: Blurb Theory, the biggest idea has to go at the end.

At Best Page Forward, all our hooks are required to end on one of three stakes:

- *Death*
- *Love*
- *Enlightenment*

We call these, appropriately, The Three Stakes, and you're probably going to get sick of me mentioning them by the time you've made it all the way through the book. Spoiler alert: This is not the only time they will apply. Let's examine them one at time.

Death

Someone's life is in danger. Maybe it's the main character's. Maybe it's their dog. Or their mom. Or their children. Or their entire race. Or the whole planet. Maybe it's even everyone in the galaxy! Whoever is at risk here, someone's gonna die if the MC blows it.

The vast majority of our hooks at Best Page Forward end in death stakes. Why? Most people fear death. And they especially fear it if someone they care about is going to die. Put somebody's life in danger, and readers want to know what will happen.

Now, literal death is always a draw. But what if no one actually is going to die? What if you're writing children's books? You can't have death stakes then, right?

Well, death can be metaphorical. If a dream dies, that's every bit as devastating. For school-aged children, being ostracized from a friend group – social death – is far more terrifying than actually dying. An unwanted divorce is a form of death. So is getting fired.

Death is the end. It's final. It closes doors. So, any sort of metaphorical death works for those stakes.

As long as *those* are the highest possible stakes. We can't forget this important rule. The *highest possible* stakes are what go at the end. Because we don't want to come down. We want to keep the tension rising.

Love

These are always the stakes in a romance, and they can work for other kinds of fiction, too. Like with death, the most obvious stakes are easy to spot: two people not getting together. In a romance novel, this is the whole plot – Person A and Person B fall in love, and we wonder if they get their happily ever after.

But this doesn't have to imply romantic love. We could put a parent's or child's love at stake. We could put a friendship at risk. If you really want to get a bit esoteric, it could be self-love on the line. All of those uses are less common than romantic love, and they may cross more comfortably into death stakes. But the point is, if things go sideways, love will not win in the end.

Enlightenment

These are the rarest and hardest stakes to nail down. They appear most often in literary fiction, women's fiction, and memoirs. The big question here is, "Will our protagonist learn something important?"

Lit- and women's-fic generally ponder deep human themes, and enlightenment stakes get tied up in how that plays out over the narrative. Many memoirs tell the story of the author's awakening to some great truth they want to share. Those are enlightenment stakes in a nutshell.

The other subgenre you often see enlightenment stakes for is the road novel. In a book about a road trip, the external journey acts as a mirror for the inner quest the MC must undergo to grow. Enlightenment stakes are pretty natural for those kinds of stories.

The Final Word

We've already discussed the importance of ending on the highest stakes/most important idea. But we can take this further. A hook really sings when not only does it end on the highest stakes but on the strongest *word*.

At Best Page Forward, we're always trying to end with a bang. If we've got death stakes, we want to end with a word that means business. Some examples:

- Doom
- Dead/Death
- Kill/Killed/Killer
- Murder/Murderer
- Die/Dying
- End
- Armageddon/Apocalypse
- Destroyed/Destroyer

That's a *very* short list. We're always looking to use a word that somehow implies death and has a good, strong sound.

It's a similar idea for love stakes:

- Love/Loved/Lover
- Romance
- Passion
- Desire

- Forever
- Happy ending/happily ever after
- Heart

All those hit romance readers right in the feels, and that's what we want. We're leaving those readers with the idea that love is in the air, and someone is gonna breathe it in and get themselves totally bewitched forever.

Enlightenment stakes are a little harder. It really depends what the exact stakes are. But here's a tip: End with the emotion or lesson the MC is grappling with. Make it the strongest synonym you can for whatever is at stake.

Showing Strength

So, what's a strong word? As a general rule, these are short, evocative, and guttural. "Antidisestablishmentarianism" is great and all, but as the longest word in English, it isn't exactly a good finisher. It takes too long to say, and it's hard to read. The same is true for "supercalifragilisticexpialidocious." In addition to just being too long, the sound of it is, after all, quite atrocious.

But "doom?" Oh, "doom" lands with a boom. (Ahem.) It's one syllable. It starts with the hard consonant, "d." And "oom" just sounds ominous.

Prepositions (Which you shouldn't be ending a sentence with anyway, right grammarians?), pronouns, and adverbs aren't great enders. They just don't have a lot of gravitas to them. They don't sock it to the reader. For example:

> *Can she track down the culprit before he kills her?*

We're ending on the highest stakes – death – which is good. But by ending the sentence with the pronoun, "her," it doesn't have the same power as:

Can she track down the killer before she winds up dead?

It amounts to the same thing. But in the second version, we're ending on the powerful word, "dead." That hits harder, which is what we want.

Hook Length

It should come as no surprise to see me tell you that a hook needs to be short. After all, our first essential element for a good blurb is brevity.

At Best Page Forward, we write all our hooks to be between 50 and 150 characters. There are two reasons for this.

First, we want the hook to be usable as Amazon ad copy. Consistent branding is an important component of effective advertising. If you use your hook in an Amazon ad, the person clicks, and the first thing they see is that hook again, you've just doubled down on the message you were trying to send. Amazon requires ad copy to be between 50 and 150 characters. So that's our standard.

Second, and perhaps more importantly, 150 characters is not a lot of room to get the idea across. That forces us to be brief. It means we've got to use the strongest, most compelling words available to us. We don't have any space to waste, and that makes us write better copy.

Keep in mind, a character isn't just a letter or number. Every piece of punctuation is a character. So is every blank space. If you restrict yourself to 150 characters or fewer, you'll soon learn to get a lot done in a short burst.

We break hooks down into three classes by the number of the sentences they are. At Best Page Forward, we frequently end the hook with a question, because it naturally invites the reader to keep exploring to find out more. But you don't need to ask a question at the end. A dramatic statement is just as effective.

Each type follows a general formula. There may be a few variations on it, but they tend to all work the same way. Let's look at each one.

. . .

The One-Sentence Hook

This hook typically opens one of two ways:

- *In a world where ...*
- *When a [PERSON] [DOES SOMETHING], will ...*

In the first version, we say something about the setting, and then either ask a question or make a statement about the stakes. For example:

> *In a world without heroes, a man who can fly will give hope to millions.*

OR

> *In a world without heroes, can a flying alien hope to save the day?*

Both of those variations paint a picture of the world thirsty for a hero, someone to give the people hope. And they name the protagonist as a man who can fly, telling us this is some sort of science fiction story. Then we make the statement – he will give hope to millions – or ask a critical question – can he save the day?

We've got stakes in each of those (although maybe the first one could sound a little direr). And we have a brief picture of the plot.

In the other template, we could do something like:

> *When the last survivor of a doomed planet arrives on Earth, can he save the country from a madman's greed?*

Lots of drama packed into that. We've got the last survivor of a doomed planet, so it's clear this guy is an alien. We also know he needs to save the country from a greedy madman. We can tell the stakes are high, and we might wonder how an alien could save people from greed.

Let's think about our three questions: What does the MC want? To save the country. What's standing in his way? A greedy madman. What happens if he fails? Well, we're a little vague there. He wants to save the country, so if he fails, presumably the country is doomed. We could probably get away with those implied consequences, especially since "greed" is such a strong word to end on. But if we were concerned we hadn't raised the stakes high enough, we could do something like:

> *When the last survivor of a doomed planet arrives on Earth, can he prevent a madman's greed from leaving millions dead?*

Now, we've for sure got death at the end. It's a single sentence that answers all three hook questions, ends on the highest possible stakes, and does it all in 119 characters. Neat, simple, and evocative.

The Two-Sentence Hook

When we've only got one sentence to work with, the number of concepts we can fit in is limited. A second sentence allows us to be more expansive. This type of hook usually follows a template like this:

- *A thing is happening. What will happen to the people involved?*
- *[A PERSON] is doing a thing. Will they be successful?*

Both variations boil down to setting up the situation and then putting something at risk. Sticking with our Superman example, we could do something like:

> *California is about to crumble into the sea. Can a man from another world prevent millions from dying?*

We've got the thing happening in the first sentence. Then, we're asking what will happen. Reviewing the three questions, the MC wants to save California, it crumbling into the sea is standing in his way, and millions will die if he fails.

The second variation might be something like:

> *He came to Earth to fight for truth, justice, and the American way. But can he stop a madman from launching a nuclear disaster?*

Once again, we've got our three questions answered. The hero wants to fight for truth, justice, and the American way. A madman is standing in his way. The consequences of failure are nuclear disaster.

If we wanted to do a two-sentence hook and end on a statement, we could get clever with something along the lines of:

> *He came to Earth to fight for truth, justice, and the American way. He's about to be buried under a madman's deadly greed.*

Here, we've got a nice play on words with the American way juxtaposed against greed. We know there are death stakes at work because the greed is deadly. But all our questions are answered again. What's in the way of truth, justice, and the American way? A madman's deadly greed. What's at stake? Death for the MC, since we say he's going to get buried.

The Three-Sentence Hook

This is the hook structure people tend to think of the most. It's not the only way to write one (as we saw above), but everyone sure seems to like it.

Human psychology is at work here. We *love* sets of three:

> *Baseball, Mom, and apple pie.*
> *The way, the truth, and the light.*
> *The past, the present, and the future.*

It just feels right in our brains when we take three ideas and put them together. Riffing on an old episode of *Gilligan's Island*, I call this phenomenon, "This, That, and the Other Thing."

For some reason, four is one thing too many. Even though popular music is almost always in 4/4 time (a testament to its power over the subconscious), three is, as the *Schoolhouse Rock* song put it, a magic number. Think of it as the Holy Hand Grenade of Antioch:

> *Three shall be the number thou shalt count, and the number of the counting shall be three. Four shalt thou not count....*

When we apply this tactic to a hook, it usually looks something like this:

- *This thing. That thing. Can they hope to survive?*
- *MC1 is this. MC2 is that. When fate brings them together, can they find love?*
- *A person. A situation. Will the person succeed?*

It's important to note here that, while the brain loves a set of three, we only want three sentences in the hook. If you try to do a set of three *and* a punchline, it doesn't work as well. We've hit four now – the number thou shalt not count. Because I majored in English, not psychology, I don't really understand why this is. But I do know that it's true, and as a professional writer, I can use this fact to my advantage.

Sticking with *Superman: The Movie*, here are another few examples of the variations above:

> *Two stolen nuclear missiles. A mad scheme to remake the West Coast. Can a man from another world save millions of lives?*

> *One is Earth's mightiest hero. The other is the greatest criminal genius of all time. When these two titans clash, can California be saved?*

> *A man faster than a speeding bullet. A missile screaming towards California. A ticking clock even he can't outrun ...*

All three of those fit our formula. What does the protagonist want? To save millions of lives, to save California, and presumably to stop the missile screaming towards California.

What's standing in his way? Two stolen nuclear missiles, the greatest criminal genius of all time, and a ticking clock even he can't outrun.

What are the consequences of failure? Millions of people die, California might not be saved, and the missile will hit California (and presumably kill millions of people).

We've got clear, life-or-death stakes each time, ending on the strongest idea. And every time, we got there in 150 characters or fewer.

There's one more hook technique, but it's generally reserved for comedy. I'll address using low stakes and *bathos* to get a laugh in the chapter on tone.

A Rose by Any Other Name

We need to take a moment to talk about names. If you'll recall from our discussion of brevity, the human mind can only retain two, *maybe three*, new ideas at once. You'll also remember that we want to keep our hooks to 150 characters or fewer, so that they are short and punchy and so they can be used as Amazon Ad copy.

When a reader first encounters your work, they are unlikely to be familiar with it, no matter how successful you become. I hate to burst anyone's bubble here, but as indie authors, we're just not on the tongue of the popular *zeitgeist*. Even if you're lucky enough to have your self-published masterpiece made into a movie starring Matt Damon and directed by Ridley Scott, it's really, really, *really* unlikely you'll be remembered as the next John Grisham or Stephen King. Give yourself a pat on the back if the names Andy Weir, Hugh Howey, or Adam Croft mean something to you, but they don't to the vast majority of people who saw the film adaptation of *The Martian*.

With all that in mind, you need to assume readers coming to your work have no idea who your characters are. So, when it comes to your hook, *don't actually tell them.*

I know that sounds about as counterintuitive an idea as you've ever heard. If they don't know the characters, why wouldn't you tell them?

Because it forces them to learn something new. That makes them think.

And we don't want potential buyers thinking. We want them engaged with the message. The more they have to think about something, the less likely they are to actually buy it.

Maybe it sounds confusing: *Who is this person, and why do I care?*

Maybe it distracts them: *Who is this person, and why—Ooh! Shiny!*

Maybe it bores them: *Who is this person? Why am I thinking about that? I'm bored. I wonder what else I can find to look at?*

My colleague at Best Page Forward, Robert Scanlon, refers to this as "reader friction." Friction, as you may recall from science class, slows things down. When we slow readers down, we lose them.

Now, if you're writing a famous public domain character like Sherlock Holmes, or an historical personage like Abraham Lincoln, then you can drop the name in if you think it will help. But this has to be someone practically everyone recognizes.

Otherwise, no proper nouns in your hooks, except well-known places. Use pronouns and descriptors instead. Go back up and look at all the hook examples in this chapter. Not one of them named a character. The only proper nouns I used were "Earth," "California," and "the West Coast." That keeps reader friction down, *and* it saved me characters – "he" is a lot shorter than "Superman."

As I've said repeatedly throughout this book, potential customers can only handle two to three new ideas at once. Don't waste one here. Save that name for the body of the blurb. It'll do better work there.

. . .

Homework

Okay, there was a *lot* to absorb in this chapter. The good news is, a lot of the techniques in this chapter will come back again. They'll feel familiar the next time (and the next, and the next ...).

You can likely guess your homework. Pick one of your chosen films/novels and write three hooks for it – a one-sentence, a two-sentence, and a three-sentence. Remember that each should provide the answer to three questions:

- What does the main character want?
- What is standing in their way?
- What are the consequences of failure?

End on the strongest concept, the highest possible stakes, and whenever possible, the strongest word.

Once you've got those knocked out, you'll be ready to dive into the actual body of the blurb! Next, we'll start with that all-important first sentence, The Gut Punch.

CHAPTER 10

THE GUT PUNCH

If you really want to get someone's attention, hit them in the stomach. Okay, don't actually do that. I'm speaking metaphorically here. The point is, while engaging in fisticuffs isn't exactly a socially acceptable greeting, it demands the recipient give you their full focus.

That's what we want to do when we open our blurb: metaphorically punch the reader in the gut.

Just as the hook is critical to getting the reader engaged and interested in the story, P1S1 is all about getting them immediately invested in the main character. That's why I've labeled it, "The Gut Punch." We want to hit the reader in the feels, and we want to do it hard and fast so that we maximize their attention. Here's how we'll do it.

Short and Sweet

I've dedicated a lot of space in the book so far to emphasizing how everything needs to be short due to the distractive age we live in. The Gut Punch takes it to a whole other level.

Your opening line should be no longer than six to ten words. That includes the first *and* last name of your protagonist.

You read that right. Six to ten words is all you get. After you name your MC, you're down to four to eight.

Okay, stop panicking. You can totally do this. I'll show you how in a moment. First, let's look at why.

We are going for maximum impact here. We want the rawest, shortest, most direct statement we can make. Strip away everything and get straight to the point. It just plain hits harder.

If you're going to punch someone in the gut, tapping them won't accomplish anything. You've got to hammer them with everything you have. The short statement gets that done.

Let's look at a comparison. First, we'll go with a longer opener:

> *After thirty years of what she thought was blissful marriage, Wendy Wilson never thought she'd get divorced.*

That paints a nice picture. We've got a woman whose life seemed idyllic, only to have the whole thing ripped out from under her.

But to use a journalism term, we've buried the lede. The point of this whole sentence is to introduce the reader to Wendy by telling them she just got a surprise divorce. So, let's get straight to it:

> *Wendy Wilson never saw the divorce coming.*

Boom! We've got everything we really need to know in just seven words. We know Wendy is getting divorced and that it was a total blindside.

You might be thinking to yourself that this sentence is missing necessary detail. Why didn't she see it coming? How long was she married? What's going on here?

The truth is, none of those details is necessary in the opening line. In fact, it's better that they're not there, because they raise questions that encourage reading further.

All we're looking for in the opener is a visceral, emotional reaction. Read that second version again:

> *Wendy Wilson never saw the divorce coming.*

That's powerful. Because it's so short, it hits like a truck. It's so much stronger than the first version, which wasted some of our reader's fleeting attention by warming them up. We softened the blow by waiting to strike.

The reason an actual gut punch is such an effective technique in a fight is that the natural state of those abdominal muscles is to be relaxed. When you hit someone by surprise, you can circumvent the body's defences, getting the force past the soft tissue and into the solar plexus. That in turn, forces the air out of the lungs, which makes it temporarily impossible to breathe. And nothing makes people panic like gasping for breath.

If you tell someone you're going to hit them in the stomach before you do it, they'll be ready. Instinctively, they'll tighten those abdominal muscles, which will make it feel like you're punching a wall. You'll still hurt them, but you won't be able to fold them in half or knock the wind out of them. They'll be able to absorb the blow.

The same is true for your P1S1. The longer you wait to get to the point, the easier it is for the reader to ignore it. The point is to get them emotionally engaged right away. If they're casually skimming, they are unlikely to be motivated enough to buy when they finish the blurb, assuming they finish it at all.

No Plot Allowed

You might have seen this coming after reading through the last section, but if you want to strip things down to just six to ten words, you don't have room for any plot. Listen, sci-fi/fantasy authors, we need to get straight to your MC's emotional journey. All that stuff that happened a thousand years ago to bring us to this point is not germane to selling the book. We want to get the reader emotionally invested in the protagonist ASAP.

Now, all y'all who may be snickering at my admonishing our speculative fiction writers need to internalize this message too. We don't have room for the plot in P1S1. Every drop of background information dilutes our emotional message.

Let's go back to the example I drafted in the previous section. Here's Version 1 again:

> ***After thirty years of what she thought was blissful marriage,*** *Wendy Wilson never thought she'd get divorced.*

Everything in bold is plot. Those add up to ten words. We're only allowed a total of ten words in The Gut Punch, and we used them *all* before we even introduced the main character! Our lede isn't just buried; it's six feet under in a coffin.

All that background information isn't unimportant in the blurb. It has a place to help us establish Wendy's character.

But that place is not P1S1.

To shock the reader into engagement, we want nothing but raw emotion. Get them straight into the character's head and heart. Don't mess around with anything else.

Strong(est) Emotion

Giving readers a feeling to lock onto is important. But when the game's on the line, you don't send your second-stringers in to win it. You want your best players with the ball in their hands.

The same is true for P1S1. We need to make sure we've got that reader's full attention. To do that, lead with the strongest possible emotion. Keep it simple and direct.

Romance authors understand this concept well. I hope they'll forgive me for putting it this way, but the emotional need of the lovers is usually pretty simplified. One of the biggest tropes in romance is the person who was badly burned once in the past and will therefore never give their heart away again. They don't believe in love. They don't trust the next person not to betray them the same way their former lover did. One of the big complications of the story is a misunderstanding where this wounded lover's fears *appear* to be confirmed.

You can criticize that for being simplistic if you like, but it works brilliantly every time. This is because romance authors, perhaps better than anyone else in the fiction game, understand that their readers want to be able to identify with the emotions of the protagonists. They want to believe love conquers all, so they want characters who have clear, understandable emotions that are validated and if necessary, conquered in the end. We'd do well to take a page from our romance colleagues and deliver a blurb that has clear, relatable motivation for the MC.

In this regard, secondary feelings will not do. We need the most powerful feelings in The Gut Punch.

Once again, let's examine that example from above:

> ~~*After thirty years of what she thought was blissful marriage,*~~
> *Wendy Wilson never thought she'd get divorced.*

I've struck through all the warmup stuff we decided to cut, leaving just the essence of Wendy's opening situation. It's a mere seven words, which is good. That'll help it be impactful.

But let's look at verbiage. Wendy "never thought she'd get divorced." We can perceive that life is changing in a way Wendy didn't expect. It feels sort of abstract, though. For one, most people don't expect to get divorced. There would be no point in getting married if you thought it would end.

As short and direct as our P1S1 is, it lacks – wait for it – punch. There's no real emotion here. We don't even know if Wendy initiated the breakup or her spouse did.

Now, let's look at my second variation on this opener:

Wendy Wilson never saw the divorce coming.

That's much stronger. We know that Wendy was taken by surprise. Because she "never saw the divorce coming," it's clear she is shocked.

We can all imagine that. Every one of us has been blindsided at least once in our lives. This is a universal, relatable feeling that immediately creates sympathy for Wendy in our hearts. That connection, that ability to relate, makes the reader want to know more. It gets them invested in the MC immediately. Because we didn't mess around and went straight for the gut, we've got their full attention.

P1S1 is a critical sentence. We want to hit hard and fast. If we do, the reader is onboard for the rest of the blurb without even realizing what's been done to them.

All in the Head

We've discussed this elsewhere, but to land an effective emotional gut punch, you've got to be inside the MC's perspective. Let's take another look at our Wendy example:

Wendy Wilson never saw the divorce coming.

That's short, impactful, and emotional. But we're still kind of outside Wendy's perspective. We're telling the reader she never saw the divorce coming. Remember the rule about no plot in the gut punch? Well, we've sort of got some plot with "divorce." So, what if we took this one step further:

Wendy Wilson is falling apart.

Wow, that hits really hard, right? Now, we don't have any plot. We just have a poor woman going to pieces. Why? We don't know. All we have is a visceral picture of a woman losing it all.

Plus, we're down from seven words to five. We came in *below* the six- to ten-word limit!

Admittedly, we have a form of the verb, "to be" – "is falling." If we played around some more, we might be able to get a stronger predicate. But it's still powerful, and we're focused slowly on the emotion, by staying inside our MC's head.

It can feel difficult to pull this off if you only have six to ten words to work with to grab readers. But a little practice will get you there. Make your MC the subject of the sentence and don't tell us about them. Show us their feelings. That's the key to driving home an emotional gut punch that will have readers focused and engaged from the get-go.

Homework

This assignment is pretty straightforward. Write a P1S1 for each of your chosen movies/books. Remember to:

- Keep it to six to ten words
- Eliminate the plot and focus solely on the character's strongest emotion
- Stay in the MC's POV

Opening lines can be tough. The good news is, following up on them is a little easier. That's what we'll look at it in the next chapter.

CHAPTER 11
THE EXPANSION

Pacing is a critically important piece of storytelling. If you move too slowly, you lose the reader to boredom. If you race forward at breakneck pace, never slowing down, you exhaust them and reduce enjoyment. There need to be rests here and there, so we can catch our breath before leaping into the next exciting twist.

The same is true for your blurb. You need a rhythm to pull the reader forward until making the purchase is pretty much the only option for them.

In The Gut Punch, we hit them hard to get their attention. Now, we're going ease off (but just a shade) so we can feed them a little extra information and build the tension.

The Expansion's Job

P1S1 was limited to six to ten words. It was all about driving the MC's initial opening emotion into the reader's mind. P1S2 will tell us more.

The expansion, as the name implies, builds on our opener. Whatever you told the reader about the protagonist in the gut punch, you have to follow up on.

I like to tell the writers at Best Page Forward, "That thing you wanted to put in P1S1 actually goes in P1S2." There are two reasons for this. First, as we discussed in Chapter 10, anything we can remove from the opener enables us to make that initial sentence rawer and more impactful. Second, we still need the information we cut; it just needs to go where it will be more effective. That's in P1S2.

Let's look at those edits I made to the sample blurb in the last chapter. After cutting and rephrasing, I had something that might look like this in my notebook:

> *~~After thirty years of what she thought was blissful marriage,~~*
> *Wendy Wilson ~~thought she'd never get divorced~~.*
>
> *Wendy Wilson ~~never saw the divorce coming~~ is falling apart.*

We cut all the information about having been married for thirty years and having been happy, because it was burying the lede in the opener and getting in the way of that visceral emotional reaction. Then we whacked out the bit about the divorce to just boil it down to the raw emotion.

But we still want all that plot detail. It's critical background information that helps set us up for the inciting incident. So, we put it in P1S2:

> *Wendy Wilson is falling apart. After thirty years of blissful marriage, learning of her husband's years-long affair and desire for a divorce devastates her.*

See how taking that information we wanted to put in P1S1 and using it instead in The expansion allows us to build on our initial opening state? The gut punch implies shock – Wendy is falling apart. In the expansion, we tell the reader more about it. They were blissfully married for thirty years, but her husband has been having an affair forever and now he wants a divorce. We've delved deeper into Wendy's situation.

Using Background to Reveal the Present

So far, I've admonished you multiple times not to focus on the plot. But we know that some of it has to go into the blurb. Otherwise, the reader won't know what's happening.

Just as I taught you to use plot to reveal emotion in Chapter 4, The Expansion can use the past to reveal the present. We need to get a sense of who this person is before we turn their world inside out with the inciting incident of the novel. And to understand who they are today, taking a quick peek back at their history helps bring their opening emotional state into focus.

Let's look at the sample P1S2 from above:

> *After thirty years of blissful marriage, learning of her husband's years-long affair and desire for a divorce devastates her.*

Our transition phrase, "After thirty years of blissful marriage," tells us about Wendy's past. The main clause in the sentence, "learning of her husband's years-long affair and desire for a divorce devastates her," shows us how she is currently feeling. We've used the past to reveal the present.

We've done it in such a way that the plot reveals emotion. That thirty years of blissful marriage is a plot point that helps explain why Wendy is devastated.

Stay Zoomed In

It's important to stay in the MC's head. Remember that we want to show instead of tell, which requires us to be inside the protag's perspective.

Our example above misses the mark by a few degrees. Take a close look at the bolded portion below:

> *After thirty years of blissful marriage,* ***learning of her husband's years-long affair and desire for a divorce*** *devastates* ***her****.*

If we recall the lessons from the chapter on agency, we can spot the problem pretty quickly. Wendy is not the subject of this sentence. I bolded "her" at the end, so we can see where she is. She's the object.

For those of you who are not grammar nerds like I am, there are three basic parts to the primary clause – subject, predicate, object. The subject is the noun which takes or gives the action. The object receives the action. Whereas the predicate is a verb that determines which of our nouns is performing which function in the sentence.

The predicate in our sample above is "devastates." It's a little tricky to spot because we also have "learning" in our primary clause. But in this case, "learning" is a gerund – an "-ing" verb functioning as a noun – that is modified by the prepositional phrase, "of her husband's years-long affair," to form the *subject* of the sentence. We've substituted "Wendy" for the pronoun, "her," and it is "her" that is receiving the action of the predicate, "devastates."

So, we're not in Wendy's POV, because she is being acted upon instead of acting. We're telling the reader about her instead of showing them how she feels. We need to rewrite a bit:

> *After three decades of blissful marriage, the fifty-two-year-old homemaker is devastated to learn her husband is leaving her for another woman.*

Now, Wendy is the subject. More precisely, "homemaker" is the subject, which we understand to mean Wendy, since it follows directly on P1S1, which establish Wendy as our POV character. (More on that in the next section.)

The predicate is, "is devastated," which isn't quite as strong as "devastates," because it's a form of the verb, "to be." But the sentence is better because Wendy has the agency and we are inside her head. We're seeing her react to the news that her husband is leaving her instead of being told what her reaction is.

By rewriting it this way, not only have we used the past to reveal the present and plot to reveal emotion, we're looking out through Wendy's eyes, which increases the reader's connection to her.

Raise the Stakes

I've written this before, but it bears repeating: Every sentence in your blurb after the first should raise the stakes. We may need to pace ourselves between full-on action and catching our breath, but the stakes need to constantly be rising. Just as in your hook you need to keep the tension increasing, the body of the whole blurb must build towards that cliffhanger. Think of it as a ladder. Each sentence is a rung. The reader climbs towards that summit of having to purchase.

The term, "the expansion," is meant to convey this. We're not just expanding on the information we provided in the gut punch. We're increasing the emotional stakes of that initial situation.

Let's take one more look at our example from above:

> *After* ***three decades*** *of blissful marriage,* ***the fifty-two-year-old homemaker*** *is devastated to learn* ***her husband is leaving her*** *for another woman.*

Each one of the bolded phrases raises the stakes from our P1S1. In The Gut Punch, we revealed that Wendy "is falling apart." By then explaining that she's been married for three decades, we can feel the other shoe about to drop. We don't know what's coming next, but leading with her falling apart, we know something bad is coming. The stakes just went up.

Next, instead of using a pronoun or Wendy's name, we've cleverly slipped in a little plot exposition by noting that she's fifty-two and a homemaker. That tells us two critically important things. Wendy married her husband when she was twenty-two, and her primary occupation has been taking care of the household. We don't know yet if they have kids that she's been raising for thirty years or if there is some other reason she's been at home. But the important part is, she doesn't have a job.

So, she's middle-aged, which is a difficult time to start over, especially if you haven't had a career. She's never really known anything other than this marriage in her adult life. Those are some pretty big stakes when we view them through the lens of P1S1 and the last part of P1S2: He's leaving her. In the gut punch, we only knew she was falling apart. However, we're told explicitly in the expansion, that her husband is leaving her. She's spent the past thirty years staying home, and at fifty-two, she's being abandoned without a job. The stakes skyrocketed in this sentence, and that's before we consider that she thought the marriage was blissful only to discover his reason for leaving is that he's having an affair.

The expansion builds on what we revealed in the gut punch to increase the emotional stakes. The content of this sentence is designed to increase what we already know from P1S1. We learn more, and the tension rises.

Homework

With a gut punch in place for each of your chosen movies/books, it's time to give the reader more. Write an expansion for each one, remembering to do the following:

- Stay inside the MC's perspective
- Keep agency with the protagonist
- Use the past to reveal the present
- Use the plot/background to reveal emotion
- Raise the emotional stakes

We've set up our main character nicely. We understand their opening emotional state, having learned where they came from to get to where they are now.

It's time to yank the rug out from under them. We're going to send our protagonist's world into chaos with the inciting incident. Join me in the next chapter to see how.

CHAPTER 12

THE INCITING INCIDENT

Everything is about to change. We've established our main character and their initial situation. Now, we're going to turn their world upside down. It's time for P1S3: the inciting incident!

What Is It Again?

Let's start with a quick reminder of what the inciting incident actually is:

- External story event
- Forces the main character out of their initial state
- And into the action of the narrative
- Occurs toward the end of Act I or the beginning of Act II

Everything in the story flows from the inciting incident. Without it, the main action of the narrative does not occur.

It's important to note that this critical piece of the plot is *not* necessarily the first thing that happens, or even the first exciting thing that happens. Whatever the inciting incident is, it forces change on *the protagonist*.

To illustrate the difference, let's take a look at the movie, *Star Wars*. The film opens with an electrifying space battle, quickly won by the bad guys. To preserve the mission, Princess Leia hides the Death Star schematics in R2-D2 and instructs him to take an escape pod to the surface of Tatooine. Leia is captured by Darth Vader, who takes her to the Death Star for interrogation.

None of this is the inciting incident. It may be the first thing that happens and is incredibly important to the movie's plot. But it's not the inciting incident because Princess Leia is not the main character. *Star Wars* does not chronicle Leia's struggle to resist Imperial torture, her desperation to warn the rebels, or her escape to deliver the plans. Those things are part of the film's action, but that is not what it is about.

Likewise, R2-D2's successful escape to Tatooine, his capture at the hands of Jawas, and his clever ruse to get the restraining bolt removed so he can continue his quest to find Obi-Wan Kenobi, is neither the central plot of the film nor its inciting incident. Once again, these things are critical to the story, and they happen early on. But R2-D2 is not the main character.

Our protagonist is Luke Skywalker. And as much as he dreams of leaving Tatooine, he's stuck working as a moisture farmer for his dull and abrasive uncle. But when he stumbles onto Princess Leia's plaintive call for help, things start to change for him.

R2-D2 shows him a portion of the message Leia recorded. He tricks Luke into removing the restraining bolt. As soon as the opportunity presents itself, R2-D2 makes a run for it.

That forces Luke to go after him if he doesn't want to get in trouble. But because of the danger of Sandpeople, he has to wait until morning. That takes him away from the farm long enough to avoid murder at the hands of Imperial troops looking for the droids. With nothing left for him on Tatooine, he is free to follow Ben Kenobi to Alderaan and begin his Jedi training.

"Help me Obi-Wan Kenobi; you're my only hope" is the inciting incident. Discovering Princess Leia's message forces Luke Skywalker out of his initial situation and into the action of the narrative. It happens not in the film's opening sequence but toward the end of the first act.

It's important to understand this distinction for blurb writing. The inciting incident goes in P1S3, because we've used the first two sentences to establish normal (whatever that looks like). Then, we turn it on its head to force the MC into action.

You have to know what the inciting incident of your novel is because it is the turning point for the story in the early narrative. It is a natural dramatic moment, which enables us to construct our book description so that the reader wants to know more.

Making It Exciting

At Best Page Forward, we used to refer to P1S3 as the first cliffhanger because that is how we use the inciting incident. We write it so that it leaves the reader hanging and makes them want to know more.

This can be one of the most difficult sentences to pull off in the whole blurb. A lot has to happen, so we need to adhere to all the rules we've set up for previous sentences. That leaves us with a quandary that looks something like this:

- We must remain inside the protagonist's head
- We must focus on showing the MC's emotional reaction to story events
- We want to give the main character agency

BUT ...

- The inciting incident is an external story event
- That acts on the protagonist
- Forcing them into the action of the narrative

All of that seems to be contradictory. How do we stay in the MC's head if we're describing an external event? How can we show emotion if the main character is being acted upon? How do we give agency if the protagonist is being forced into the narrative?

To do all this, we need to go back to a concept we introduced in Chapter 4. We need to use plot to reveal emotion.

The first part is easy. Whatever the inciting incident is will be our plot information. For example:

> *But when he stumbles across a plaintive cry for assistance from a beautiful woman ...*

We have a clear plot point here. Luke stumbles across the cry for help. Next, we need to reveal his emotional reaction.

> *... the would-be hero is desperate to help.*

"Is desperate" gives us Luke's emotional POV. Adding "to help" makes it clear that this "would-be hero" is sparked into action.

The cliffhanger comes in the shock. While I haven't composed the first two sentences of this sample *Star Wars* blurb, we can safely assume that, if I followed the Best Page Forward formula, I've established Luke as bored with life and yearning for adventure. When he stumbles across a beautiful woman in trouble, he'll be very motivated to leave that dull existence behind to pursue a rescue mission.

The Three Stakes (Again)

To have a cliffhanger, something has to be at risk. We have to leave our hero in trouble, so the reader will want to know what happens next.

In terms of the inciting incident, the status quo is either threatened or destroyed. The MC starts in one place, and then, as a result of the inciting incident, their comfortable existence is threatened. Luke Skywalker may dream of adventure, but he's basically a good kid, who does what he's told. Moisture farming sucks, but he won't transfer his application to the academy ahead of the harvest because he knows his uncle needs him.

“Look, I can’t get involved,” he tells Ben, when the retired Jedi Knight begs him to come to Alderaan.

He may *want* to go rescue the princess and fight the Empire, but he’s afraid to. He has responsibilities that he hides behind to resist the call to adventure. He hates his life, but it’s also comfortable and safe.

The inciting incident threatens it. When Luke hears Princess Leia’s plea, he feels compelled to do something. But he wants to be able to help without having to risk his position.

“I can take you as far as Anchorhead,” he offers. “You can get a transport there to Mos Eisley or wherever you’re going.”

Luke feels threatened by the inciting incident. He’s on the horns of a dilemma, and the external event of the princess’s message is forcing him out of his comfortable place.

We need more in our P1S3 than a simple story event that our MC reacts to. We need a threat.

That brings us back to the three stakes we discussed in the chapter on hooks. If we’re going to cliffhang the reader, we need to put something at risk – death, love, or enlightenment.

Death

- The character’s life is in danger
- Someone else’s life is in danger
- Everyone’s life is in danger
- Someone has died
- Everything the character has achieved may be ruined

Love

- An attractive person may be the answer to the character’s needs

- An attractive person threatens to cause the MC to reconsider their personal code against relationships
- A dark secret changes the perception the MC has of a loved one
- The MC suddenly sees a loved one or an attractive person they've resisted in a new light

Enlightenment

- Something changes the character's point of view
- The character discovers something that they've always believed to be true is wrong or a lie
- An unforeseen event disrupts the character's life

Your inciting incident should follow one of those ideas. Whatever the stakes – death, love, or enlightenment – they have somehow threatened the MC's comfortable existence.

You'll recall that, at Best Page Forward, all hooks must end with one of those three stakes. We also require every P1S3 to conclude with those high stakes. Like every other sentence in the blurb, we want to end with the biggest idea. Remember, each sentence should raise the tension higher than it was in the previous one.

To get our inciting incident right for the blurb, to make it work as a cliffhanger, it has to raise the stakes from P1S2 and end on death, love, or enlightenment.

Let's have another look at Luke Skywalker's discovery of Princess Leia's message. We left things thus:

> *But when he stumbles across a plaintive cry for assistance from a beautiful woman, the would-be hero is desperate to help.*

We've got our inciting incident of the stumbling across the plaintive cry for assistance, and we can see Luke reacting emotionally. But we're not exactly ending on the highest possible stakes. He's "desperate to help." But neither Luke nor his comfortable situation is under threat in this sentence. So, we need to do a little rewriting and reorganizing. What if we did something like this:

> *But the daydreaming farm boy is stunned when he stumbles across a beautiful woman's desperate plea for help.*

Though all the concepts from the previous draft are still there, this is a very different sentence. We've moved Luke's emotional reaction to the front of the sentence and the inciting incident itself to the back. By flipping the order of things, we're ending with death stakes. Now the sentence isn't about Luke wanting to help the anonymous woman in the message; it's about her life being in danger. We don't know the exact nature of the trouble she's in. But we know her plea is desperate. If we wanted to ramp up the danger a little more, we could add something like, "... to prevent the rebellion's destruction." Now, that sense of death is even stronger. But the point is, we've ended the sentence and the paragraph on the highest possible stakes.

And yet, we've still used them to reveal emotion. Luke is "stunned" when he discovers the video fragment. He's a "daydreaming farm boy" – not the type of person who expects to receive a plaintive cry for help from a beautiful princess. And his emotional reaction as well as the inciting incident itself threaten his status quo.

That makes the reader want to know more, which is critical because P1S3 has another important job: Push them into the next paragraph.

In the heyday of print journalism, papers would be folded in half for display on newsstands. The most important information was near the top of the page, or "above the fold," to entice the reader to pick it up and learn more. (That's also why frontpage stories never finished on the front page. You'd have to turn to the back to find out the rest, which usually meant you had to buy it.)

On the Amazon sales page, a similar dynamic is at work. Unless your blurb is only a sentence or two long, it won't all fit on the "front page." Amazon arbitrarily cuts it off after a few lines, forcing the reader to click "Read More" to continue.

So, we want at least part of our inciting incident "above the fold," and we need it to be exciting enough that it pushes the reader into the next paragraph. They click "Read More," because they're interested enough to find out what happens next. High stakes are the means to make that happen.

Homework

Let's go back to the homework you did for Chapter 8. Have a look at P1S3. Now that you have a clearer distinction between the story's opening events and its inciting incident, did you identify the correct plot point for each book or movie? If so, great! If not, take a moment to figure out what it actually is.

With your inciting incidents lined up, write a P1S3 for each film or novel. Remember that:

- It is an external story event
- That acts on the protagonist
- Forcing them into the action of the narrative

But when we write that sentence, we want to:

- Remain inside the protagonist's head
- Focus on showing the MC's emotional reaction to the inciting incident
- Give the main character agency

AND:

- Threaten the protagonist's status quo
- End on the highest possible stakes
- Push readers over the fold

Congratulations! We've gotten through our first paragraph! Have a mini-celebration and then join me in the next chapter as we explore how to get from the inciting incident into the next portion of the story.

CHAPTER 13
THE BRIDGE

Paragraphs are natural breaks, and as a result, they're an opportunity for readers to reset their attention. That can be a major problem for a book blurb. Remember, that any chance for distraction can lead to the person navigating away from our sales page instead of finishing the copy and clicking the buy button. We need to make sure we get them from that cliffhanger ending of P1 and into the next paragraph, where we'll continue to build the tension.

And that's what this chapter is all about.

The Bridge's Job

We call P2S1, "the bridge," because it's a transfer point. Think of this part of the blurb as crossing a river. On one bank, we have the inciting incident and the chaos it is wreaking on the MC's world. On the other side, we have the protagonist's new situation or emotional state *as a result of* the inciting incident. P2S1 is going to get us there smoothly and quickly, so that, by the time our crossing is complete, the stakes have gone up again.

The bridge is really comprised of two pieces, both of which are essential to accomplishing its mission. These are:

- The Transition
- The New Emotional State

We'll examine each one in-depth.

The Transition

We've already discussed transitions a bit in previous chapters. A transition can use the plot to reveal emotion, like in the inciting incident. Or it can use the past to reveal the present like in the expansion.

As a general rule, the transition in the bridge is:

- The front half of the sentence
- A plot point

For the most part, your transition is the first thing we read in P2S1. The reason for this is pretty simple: We need to re-hook the reader. They very likely have had to click "Read More" to get here, which means their head was out of the flow for a second. Even if they have the full description in front of them before they start reading, we still need to overcome that line break. A nice, hooky transition helps re-establish what's happening and consequently, their interest.

Your best friends in this situation are "-ing" verbs. They show action, which helps create movement in the mind. Remember, we're crossing a bridge here and raising the stakes. We need that sense of rising tension. To do that, take a good, descriptive verb and slap an "-ing" on it.

- **Attacking** the bunker at dawn ...
- **Following** the clues to a shady warehouse ...
- **Teaming** up with the gorgeous *femme fatale* ...

See how that works? Each one of those phrases begins with an "-ing" verb and introduces a plot point. As a result, they create a transition from where we left the protagonist at the end of P1S3 and move us towards the next part of the sentence.

The New Emotional State

Remember, we want to use plot to reveal emotion. If the transition phrase was plot-oriented, we want to show how the character feels about it. Since the goal of the bridge is to demonstrate the change the MC is undergoing as a result of the inciting incident, this part of the sentence is critical.

Now, we can't forget our protagonist needs agency. This may be where we show what their reaction is, but they still need to be in control of what's happening. Ensure your protagonist is the subject of the sentence. They can't have agency if they're the object.

Let's finish those samples from above:

- ... Helen hopes she is finally striking the final blow for freedom.
- ... Xander fears what he finds confirms his worst suspicions.
- ... Jordan fights falling for a woman she's sure can't be trusted.

In every one of those examples, our MC was the subject. Helen hopes. Xander fears. Jordan fights.

We've also revealed an emotional state in each of them. "Helen hopes" and "Xander fears" are emotional. "Jordan fights" is not, but we've attached the adverbial phrase, "falling for a woman...." What is she fighting? Falling in love with a woman she's sure can't be trusted. The sentence implies our *femme fatale* has got her hooks into Jordan, and we can see she's worried about what that means.

Reversing the Polarity

While generally the plot point comes first and the emotional revelation second, you *can* do it in the opposite order. Sometimes, it makes more sense to show an emotional reaction to the inciting incident and then the plot situation that results. For example:

> *Wishing his master were still alive to guide him, Benjamin sets off into the jungle to find the missing artifact.*

Everything's in the opposite order here. Our new emotional state is in the transition – "Wishing his master were still alive to guide him ..." In that sentence, "Wishing" is an emotional verb. The master is no longer alive, so he can't provide Benjamin guidance. Our hero yearns for something he can't have that would be directly relevant to the situation.

Then, our plot event is in the back half of the sentence – "Benjamin sets off into the jungle to find the missing artifact." That's all story. There's no emotion there.

But we've still accomplished all our objectives. We've used plot (Benjamin sets off to find the artifact) to reveal emotion (he wishes his master were here to guide him). And we've built a bridge from P1S3 to get that new situation set up. We might have done it in reverse order, but it all makes perfect sense, reads well, and keeps the browser engaged, wondering what will happen next.

Additionally, our stakes continued to rise. Benjamin has left the safety of wherever he was to enter the jungle to seek out this missing artifact. By moving into the narrative, the stakes have naturally gone up. Plus, he's wishing his master was there to guide him. That creates uncertainty and worry that he won't be good enough. Benjamin can't be sure he's doing the right thing because his mentor can't confirm or refute his choices. He's out in the jungle without a safety net, hoping he did the right thing. That raises the stakes as well.

The bridge does, if you'll excuse the pun, a lot of heavy lifting. It gets us from our first paragraph to the new situation and sets us up for the big swerve coming up next. But let's not get ahead of ourselves. We need some practice before moving on.

. . .

Homework

It's time to pull out your chosen books or movies again. Write a Bridge for each one. Experiment with using the traditional order and the reversed version. Remember our goals:

- Use plot to reveal the MC's new emotional state
- Re-hook the reader, so they don't navigate away
- Keep the agency with the protagonist

Next up, we'll examine the role of complications and how they'll raise the stakes even further.

CHAPTER 14
THE COMPLICATION

So far, we've established our main character's emotional state. We've forced them out of their comfortable world and into the action of the narrative. We've established their new situation.

Now, it's time to make things hard.

The line between a character's goals and their starting point never runs straight. Nor is it ever smooth. Something always gets in the way. In P2S2, we're going to let the reader know what that is.

Running Interference

Put simply, the job of the complication is to let the reader know something could thwart the MC's goal. Maybe it's the antagonist. Maybe it's a dearth of clues or leads. Maybe it's the character's own self-doubt. Whatever it is, it has an excellent chance to bring our protagonist to failure. The stakes need to go up, because now, not only is everything on the line, the main character may blow it.

We're going to use all the techniques we've learned so far. We want to use plot to reveal emotion. We want to have a transitional phrase that leads into a big uh-oh. And we want the strongest concept – and preferably, the strongest word – at the end.

Let's pretend we're writing a blurb for James Cameron's seminal 1984 sci-fi thriller, *The Terminator*. In our first paragraph, we established Sarah Connor as a waitress who can barely balance her checkbook or get the orders right during the lunch rush. She can't get a boyfriend. And then without warning, a strange man shows up in a bar and tries to kill her.

In our second paragraph, she learns that the badass dude with the guns is actually a cyborg from the future sent back in time to murder her before she can give birth to the guy who will actually lead humanity to victory over the machines. Now, we're set up to throw a major complication at her.

> *But with the dread machine stalking her every move and being all but impervious to contemporary weapons, Sarah fears both she and the human race are about to run out of time.*

We have everything we need here. We have a transition phrase that gives us some key plot information – the Terminator is stalking her every move, and it is nearly invincible. We have a main phrase that reveals emotion – Sarah fears she and the human race are dead. And we're ending on high stakes – she and humanity are about to run out of time – which is a nice, little *double entendre*, since *The Terminator* is a time-travel film.

The Three Stakes (Yet Again)

We've been over this on multiple occasions already. We need to have the highest possible stakes at the end of our sentence. In our hook, in the inciting incident, and now in the complication, we want to end on death, love, or enlightenment. After all, if we're going to threaten the MC with failure, it has to be costly. If it's not that big a deal, then it won't matter to our protagonist. More importantly, it won't matter to readers. We need their concern if we want to get the sale.

The Terminator example above ends on death stakes. "Run out of time" makes it pretty clear that everyone is gonna die, especially since we've established earlier in the blurb that the thing chasing Sarah is an unstoppable killing machine. We could have gone with "are doomed" instead, since "doomed" is a nice, hard word that is rife with awful implications. But as I noted above, "out of time" give us some fun wordplay in a blurb for a movie about people traveling to the past to change the future.

What about love stakes? If instead of Sarah's POV, the blurb featured the perspective of her overmatched protector, Reese, we could do something like:

> *And as the diabolical killing machine closes in, Reese fears he won't be good enough to save the mother of the future – the woman he has come to love....*

Here, we've put poor Reese in double-jeopardy. Not only is he likely to fail in his mission to protect Sarah from termination, he's in love with her. That failure will be so much worse.

The Terminator doesn't lend itself all that well to enlightenment stakes, so let's switch to something a little less doom-and-gloom. *The Muppet Movie* is a road film, which tend to be about inner journeys of personal growth. For the complication in Jim Henson's 1979 classic, we might have something like:

> *But with so many people depending on him despite the odds, Kermit fears their faith has been grossly misplaced.*

Once again, we have our plot in the transition phrase by referencing the whole gang of Muppets who have hitched their carts to Kermit's star. But our froggy hero is having grave doubts about whether he can pull it off (which come to a head after Fozzie's Studebaker breaks down in the desert). Our main phrase reveals emotion (Kermit fears), and it's about enlightenment. Everyone has put their trust in him, a role he's not taken on before. He isn't sure he's up to the challenge. The clever thing about the example above is that Kermit is having a crisis of faith over his friends' faith in him.

We need these high stakes at the end of P2S2 because it will set us up for the cliffhanger. We'll look at that in greater depth in the next chapter.

Getting Personal

We've discussed elsewhere the importance of making the reader care about the character. We want them to sympathize with and root for our MC. For that to occur, they have to worry about what will happen to our protagonist. Will they succeed or fail?

Well, the reader will care a lot more about the character's fate if the protagonist themselves cares. The best way to accomplish that is by making things personal for them.

Let's take another look at that first example for *The Terminator*:

> *But with the dread machine stalking her every move and being all but impervious to contemporary weapons, Sarah fears both she and the human race are about to run out of time.*

Now, Sarah is under threat. Both *she* and the human race are running out of time. But what if our heroic Ms. Connor doesn't have a very strong survival instinct? What if she thinks she's a hot mess, and the human race needs a better savior? Weariness and desperation might be enough to make her give up, and saving the entire species is kind of an abstract idea that's hard to really visualize in the moment.

So, although Sarah's life is at risk, these might not actually be the highest possible stakes, since they're not personal. What if we made a small change along the lines of:

> *But with the dread machine stalking her every move and being all but impervious to contemporary weapons, Sarah fears both the human race and her unborn child are about to run out of time.*

Now, these stakes are intensely personal. The human race is still in great danger. But so is a child she hasn't even conceived yet. It's not just humanity's future on the line; it's Sarah's, too. Her legacy, her bloodline, a child she presumably would come to love, are all at risk.

We've emphasized this by putting her future baby *second* in the sentence. Remember, we want to put the most important thing at the end of the sentence. To make these stakes really personal for Sarah, the future of her child is *more important* than the future of humanity.

If a thing matters intensely to the main character, the readers will feel this and wonder what will happen. That tension makes them want to know more and gets them one step closer to clicking the Buy Now button.

Homework

You know what to do. Look at your chosen books or movies. What's a major complication that's standing in the way of the main character? There are probably several. Choose one that occurs roughly in the first half of the story but definitely has an impact on the outcome.

Now, write those P2S2s for each of them. Don't forget to end on the highest possible stakes and make them personal.

We only have one piece of the main body left – the cliffhanger. This is where we'll get those readers really excited and needing to know more. When you finished your homework, turn the page to join me for the big finish!

CHAPTER 15
THE CLIFFHANGER

We've thrown the term, "cliffhanger," around several times over the course of our discussion. Let's take a moment to explore what it means.

The word comes from the old movie serials of the Thirties, Forties, and Fifties. Before the advent of streaming services that let you watch an entire season or even an entire series in a matter of hours, serialized shows were broadcast at a specific time, once a week. Prior to TVs being everywhere, these programs were shown in movie theaters, usually during Saturday afternoons to entertain young people.

Well, you had to pay to get into the movie theater just like you do today. Less scrupulous marketers from the mid-twentieth century wanted to make sure that captive audience kept coming back week after week. Unlike a modern TV show, where advertising or subscription fees pay to keep it on the air, serials were dependent on ticket sales to make their money. That meant they had to make sure people were lured back each Saturday.

Since most of those programs were adventure-themed, it was easy to end an episode with the hero in danger and his fate in doubt. If you wanted to know what happened to him, you had to come back next week. A favored technique was to have the hero hanging from a cliff or other high surface with no obvious means of escape.

Hence, "cliffhanger." As well as the phrase, "leave him hanging."

In our blurbs, we want to apply a similar technique, albeit a bit more ethically than those serials with a never-ending skein of uncertainty. We want to leave the protagonist's fate in doubt. The only way to find out is to actually buy the book and read it.

We've had cliffhangers in several places in our blurb to this point. But now, we're going to hit them with *the* cliffhanger.

Riddle Me This

The cliffhanger is always posed as a question. We're going to straight-up ask the reader if the MC will succeed or fail. By putting this question in their head, they'll be unable to escape wondering what the answer is. If we've done our job right, building the tension and the stakes as we go, they should feel compelled to find out.

At Best Page Forward, we nearly always begin the cliffhanger with either "can" or "will." One of those words is going to put us in position to query the reader.

> *Will Ralphie outwit his mother for the greatest Christmas present ever?*

> *Can Ralphie escape the impenetrable web of the mother's BB-gun block?*

In both versions, we've asked a key question about whether or not Ralphie's ultimate goal will be thwarted. Will he outwit his mother? Can he escape the BB-gun block? There's only one way to find out. Click "Buy Now."

There are a couple variations on this basic approach. We can go for the short, to-the-point question like above, which is usually what we do at Best Page Forward. Economy of words and all that.

But sometimes, we can make things more dramatic by creating an either-or proposition.

> *Can Ralphie convince his mother he won't shoot his eye out, or is he doomed to be the only kid who* doesn't *get what he wants for Christmas?*

By offering a sort of compare-and-contrast set of possible outcomes, we can make the stakes seem even more dire. (This would work especially well for *A Christmas Story* if we've spent our two paragraphs establishing how desperately Ralphie wants the air rifle and how firmly his mother opposes it. Anyone who's ever been a kid who wants something Mom has said no to will feel the impossibility of Ralphie's quest.)

Another variation is to open with a transition phrase that further raises the stakes from where we left them at the end of the complication:

> *With every dream he's ever had on the line, can Ralphie convince his mother he won't shoot his eye out?*

We've raised the tension in this version by throwing in the transition phrase at the beginning. Just asking, "Can Ralphie convince his mother he won't shoot his eye out," doesn't have a lot of gravitas by itself. But by opening with a phrase claiming every dream he's ever had is at stake, now this impossible task seems gravely important.

The Three Stakes Once More

I told you you'd get sick of hearing about this. Here we are one more time with the three stakes that Best Page Forward rules say we must end on. When we get to the cliffhanger, we must have the highest, biggest, baddest stakes yet. Whether we're working with death, love, or enlightenment, we need to be at the absolute apex of the tension. Everything has been leading to this. We have to deliver.

> *Can Ralphie escape the impenetrable web of the mother's BB-gun block to save Christmas?*

Christmas is at stake here? *All* of Christmas?

You bet it is. For nine-year-old Ralphie, this quest has taken on the greatest importance of his entire life. Nothing could be more critical than unwrapping an official Red Ryder range model air rifle on Christmas morning. If he can't find the answer to this terrible quandary, his life might as well be over.

(Among the genius things in *A Christmas Story* is Jean Shepherd's narration. His melodramatic delivery makes us believe that, for Ralphie, this really is life and death.)

> *Will Ralphie unwrap that coiled-steel beauty on Christmas morning and earn his parents' love?*

This particular example is a little convoluted. There's not a lot of evidence to support the premise that Ralphie has tied getting what he wants for Christmas to love from his parents. But again, what makes *A Christmas Story* work is Shepherd's ability to tell the tale from a kid's point of view. We feel Ralphie's pain and joy and desire intensely as the film progresses. There has never been a kid who didn't think, "If you loved me, you'd do it," at least once in their life.

Suggesting that love – the ultimate love of his parents – is at risk isn't that much of a stretch for this particular movie. Those are high stakes, indeed. Will Ralphie discover his parents don't actually love him? That would be pretty awful and would definitely ruin Christmas!

> *Can Ralphie prove he won't shoot his eye out and experience true Christmas joy?*

Now, we have an enlightenment (of sorts) on the line. Our young man has to prove he won't be wearing a patch the rest of his life. If he can do it, he'll know true joy. Those are pretty high stakes for a nine-year-old.

All by Itself

The cliffhanger stands alone. Where we previously had a three-sentence and a two-sentence paragraph, the cliffhanger gets no help from anything. It is out there all by itself.

That's for emphasis. Just as we sometimes use fragments to add drama, putting our final question out on its own helps really drive it home. This is the big question. Will the hero succeed or fail? By leaving it out on an island, we make it hit harder. That deepens the emotional impact and increases the likelihood of a sale.

Homework

It's time for the big finish. Write a cliffhanger for each of your chosen movies or books. Don't forget to:

- Pose it as a question
- Ask if the hero will succeed
- Raise the stakes to the highest they can possibly go
- Set it off from P2 in its own paragraph

Congratulations! You've learned how to write a fantastic fiction blurb the Best Page Forward Way!

But we're not done yet. So far, we've only summarized the book. Now, we need to sell it. That's what we'll focus on in Chapter 16.

CHAPTER 16
THE SELLING PARAGRAPH

We've spent the last six sentences plus the hook getting the reader excited about our novel. With everything primed, it's time to sell.

As I mentioned briefly back in Chapter 8, the selling paragraph is comprised of two sentences. Both of them are designed to let the reader know that this book is for them. Each follows a specific formula (which makes them easy to write), and they both help confirm for the reader that this is indeed something they want to own.

What It Is

First, we're going to tell readers exactly what they'll be buying. The formula for What It Is goes like this:

> *[BOOK TITLE] is the [ADJECTIVE] [NUMBER] book in the [SERIES TITLE] [GENRE] series.*

Everything in caps and brackets is where you insert the particulars for your novel. So, for example:

> The Fellowship of the Ring *is the engrossing first book in* The Lord of the Rings *epic fantasy series.*

Notice how this is all just a simple statement. We're telling the reader what it is. Think about each piece of SPS1 as a statement answering a question.

- What is the title of your book?
- *The Fellowship of the Ring*
- Is this book part of a series?
- Yes, it's Book 1
- What is the title of the series?
- *The Lord of the Rings*
- What genre is this series?
- An epic fantasy series

See how that single sentence neatly answers all those important questions? As the name implies, SPS1's job is to tell the reader what the book is. In this case, *The Fellowship of the Ring* is the engrossing first book of an epic fantasy series titled, *The Lord of the Rings*.

"But wait, Phoebe!" you say. "What if my series features books with different main characters and can be read in any order?"

Good question. We see this a lot in romance series, wherein all the books are set in the same location, but each story is a different pair of lovers getting together. In that case, you're going to modify your What-It-Is as follows:

> *[BOOK TITLE] is the [ADJECTIVE] [NUMBER]* ***standalone*** *book in the [SERIES TITLE] [GENRE] series.*

I've bolded the change. Notice that all you've done is add the word, "standalone." We still want all the other elements. We need the book title, of course. And readers like knowing a book is part of a series, because if they like this one, then they'll know there are more novels they can read set in the same universe/by the same author. Even though this is a standalone, you're promising them more good stuff in the future.

"But wait, Phoebe!" you cry. "My book isn't in a series at all. I only write standalone books."

Not to worry. We've got that covered, too. Modify the formula thus:

> *[BOOK TITLE] is **a/an** [ADJECTIVE] [GENRE] **novel**.*

Once again, I've bolded the changes. First, we have to go from "the" to "a" or "an" since we're not going to tell folks what number in the series it is. Second, we've shortened everything down to just make it about this singular book. For example:

> Where the Crawdads Sing *is an enthralling women's fiction novel.*

Short, simple, and to the point. We have our title and our genre.

Speaking of which, I am aware that a novel, by its very definition, is fiction. In the example above, we're using "women's fiction" as a genre marker. If you're worried about reader confusion on something like that, you could hyphenate "women's fiction," to make it obvious that it is a compound word modifying "novel" as a whole – "... an enthralling women's-fiction novel." Or you could substitute "book" for "novel." Or you could reword a bit to write, "an enthralling work of women's fiction."

The bottom line here is that we want still to designate the genre, so that it is clear what the reader is getting when they make the purchase.

"Hold on, Phoebs," you protest. "*My* book is a cross-genre fusion. What do I do now?

In some cases, you may be able to name both. For example, you could label an espionage thriller set in a fantasy world as, "a fantasy-thriller mashup."

As a general rule, though, you're better off naming the primary genre. Which one is that? Ask yourself this question:

If I walked into a bookstore, what section would my novel be in?

Most of the time this is pretty simple. Think about what typical readers of each genre accept in their books. Would fantasy readers accept thrilling secret agents and doomsday devices in their lands of make-believe? Handled correctly, they probably would. Would fans of Ian Fleming, Lee Childs, and Mark Dawson be happy with dragons and wizards in their books? Probably not. Because of that, our fantasy-thriller mashup would definitely be shelved in the fantasy section.

Remember: We don't want to confuse readers or overcomplicate things when we're trying to sell. Keep it simple. Go with the primary genre and leave it at that.

Why You Want It

Our second sentence in the selling paragraph is all about closing the deal. We've spent time getting the reader excited about the content. We've told them what sort of novel this is. Now, we want to tell them why they'll like it. Here's the formula:

> *If you like X, Y, and Z, then you'll love [AUTHOR NAME]'s [ADJECTIVE] tale/story/adventure/thrill-ride/etc.*

First, we want to name some things that are in the book. That's our X, Y, and Z. So, to return to our "Fellowship" example:

> *If you like heroic quests, deep bonds of friendship, and courage in the face of terrifying danger ...*

See how each one of these things is something that can be found within the pages of *The Fellowship of the Ring*? They're story tropes the reader is likely seeking by browsing for epic fantasy books, and they are ones that can be found inside this particular novel.

A lot of authors like to use similar books here instead of tropes. For example, "If you like *A Game of Thrones*, *The Way of Kings*, and *The Name of the Wind*, then you'll love ..." The thinking here is that, by comparing your book to others in the genre readers are apt to have liked, they'll also want to buy your novel.

At Best Page Forward, we don't recommend this for a number of reasons. First, you're effectively recommending other series/authors. By mentioning George R. R. Martin, for example, you've pulled the reader's attention from your book/series to his. We've found it is much better to keep them focused on you.

Independent authors simply can't compete on the same playing field as international bestsellers that may have had a TV series or movie adaptation. Now, you might argue that the likes of Lindsay Buroker, Mark Dawson, and K.F. Breene would disagree with me. They're all six- and seven-figure indies.

But the truth is, those folks have leveled the playing field for themselves by writing to-market fiction and using guerilla marketing tactics to outmaneuver the trad houses. You can make a lot of money at the indie author game, but you can't do it by using the trad-house playbook. Keep readers' minds in *your* world instead of better-known ones.

Additionally, there is a subset of people out there who have snide mindsets when it comes to comparison. They may think, "Oh, you're not as good as George R.R. Martin. No one is. I'm not going to buy your book out of spite, because you had the gall to compare yourself to my literary hero."

(Frankly, people like this need a strong dose of humility they are unlikely to ever get. But it's best not to feed the trolls. Don't give these folks ammunition.)

Of course, you can also have the opposite effect if the person *didn't* like the book you mention. "Ugh! I hated *A Game of Thrones*! No way am I buying this!"

Making comparisons with similar works can have upsides. But there are potential pitfalls, too. Instead of citing others, focus on tropes that are in *your* novel. Those will help identify it as a book the reader will enjoy.

Speaking of which, we now want to hit the back half of the sentence. This is where we are going to confirm this is for them:

> *... then you'll love J.R.R. Tolkien's sweeping adventure.*

Here, we made sure to get our author name in, so the reader can identify more books. If they've read Tolkien before – perhaps, *The Hobbit* – then they'll be further intrigued. If not, we've planted a seed for the future. We've used some genre language (more on that in Chapter 20) to help further confirm this is the type of book the reader is looking for. In this instance, "sweeping adventure" is likely to hit all the right notes for an epic fantasy browser.

The whole sentence would read:

> *If you like heroic quests, deep bonds of friendship, and courage in the face of terrifying danger, then you'll love J.R.R. Tolkien's sweeping adventure.*

We've identified three tropes they are likely to enjoy – heroic quests, deep bonds of friendship, and courage in the face of terrifying danger – and essentially told them they'll find them inside.

The entire Selling Paragraph reads:

> The Fellowship of the Ring *is the engrossing first book in* The Lord of the Rings *epic fantasy series. If you like heroic quests, deep bonds of friendship, and courage in the face of terrifying danger, then you'll love J.R.R. Tolkien's sweeping adventure.*

We've told them what it is and why they will like it. Mission accomplished!

. . .

A Word about Adjectives

Some authors are uncomfortable with tooting their own horn. They think it's embarrassing, or they worry people will think they're self-aggrandizing and not buy.

It's understandable. Being an artist is a wild series of contradictions. We want to be recognized for the things we create. But we fear people criticizing us. We work through terribly private emotions in our stories, and then put them out in public for anyone to consume. It can feel a bit like standing naked in the middle of downtown and declaring to all the world how good you look.

Here's the thing: Readers don't really know that authors write their own ad copy. While they are generally aware of the existence of indie publishing and the fact that it has incited a revolution for writers, most of them can't tell an indie book from a trad one. They just like to read good stories, and they don't really care who wrote them or how they were published.

(Indeed, this is the thing trad houses cannot get their minds around.)

Unlike a traditionally published author, you do not have a marketing department thinking up praise for your work. *You* are the marketing department for your indie-author business (as well as every other department you haven't outsourced).

Don't be afraid to puff up that book. Make those bold claims. Why? Because they help sell.

Now, you're best off shying away from adjectives that are solely value judgments. Words like:

- Brilliant
- Triumphant
- Stunning
- Amazing
- Incredible

That's a short list. You can probably think of some others. But the common denominator is that these words generally only say, "This is a damned good book!"

Instead, we want to find words that can also be used to accurately describe the contents. Words like:

- Thrilling
- Exciting
- Moving
- Emotional
- Pulse-pounding

Technically, these are all value judgments, too. But they also work on describing the content of the book. If you've written an action novel, there are likely to be many thrilling or exciting scenes. If you've written a powerful literary novel, there's a strong possibility the scenes are moving or emotional. Adjectives like this are excellent choices, because they accurately describe what's inside instead of just saying, "This is good."

A third type of adjective for your SP is one that describes the reading experience:

- Absorbing
- Gripping
- Page-turning
- Enthralling
- Engrossing

Once again, these are value judgments, but they are discussing what it is like to read the book rather than telling the reader how good it is. A "gripping" book is one that is tough to put down. (Indeed, "unputdownable" has become a word to describe page-turning fiction.)

This is a solid sales tactic, too. Readers love to get lost in a good book. Letting them know this is the kind of story where that will happen is a great sales technique.

Remember, the goal of the selling paragraph is to tell the reader what sort of book this is and confirm for them it's one they'll like. So, make sure the adjectives you use serve this purpose.

Homework

This exercise might be a little trickier than the others if you're using movies or if all the samples you chose are standalones. If you're working on a film, pretend it's a book for this chapter's homework. If you don't have any series choices, act like one of them is, make up a series name for it, and do the exercise that way.

Your task is to go through your chosen books/movies and write selling paragraphs for each one. Remember:

- The first sentence tells the reader what it is
- Book/movie name
- Which number in the series it is
- The name of the series
- What genre it is
- The second sentence tells the reader why they'll like it
- Name three tropes that feature in the story
- Name the author (or director for a film)

If you can believe it, we only have one piece of the puzzle left to fit! In the next chapter, we'll discuss the all-important call to action. Once you've finished your assignment, meet me there!

CHAPTER 17
THE CALL TO ACTION

Everything is in place now. The reader is excited about your novel. We've told them what it is and confirmed for them they will like it. They're ready to get it.

So, it's time to tell them to do it!

Definition

The call to action, or "CTA" as it's abbreviated in the ad game, is basically a command, spurring the customer to do something. In blurb writing, we want them to buy the book. So, we're going to straight-up tell them to do that.

Remember, we live in the Age of Distraction. Amazon only cares about enticing shoppers to buy *something*. They don't really care what it is. They just want happy customers putting money into the company's coffers.

That means there are ads for *other* products, especially other books, on *your* sales page. Imagine: A reader makes it all the way to the end of your description, they're excited to get the book, so they—Ooh! Shiny!

It happens. So, we want to make sure we've firmly told them what to do to help prevent them from navigating away. If the command to buy is in the front of their mind, they're a lot more likely to click the "Buy Now" button than they are to follow the trail of whichever shiny object Amazon teased them with at the bottom of your sales page.

It's Okay to Ask for a Sale

I've had authors tell us a blurb we've sent them amounts to "sleazy salesmanship" because of the CTA. I've also heard authors around the Interwebz say they would never tell someone to buy their book for what amounts to the same reason: It turns readers off.

Let's dispel this myth right now. Readers are not turned off by you asking them to buy your book. Unless they are freebie-seekers, they *expect* to have to buy the novel if they want to read it. I'm just gonna repeat this so you can be sure to digest it:

Readers ***expect*** *to have to pay to read your book.*

A lot of authors (by which I mean practically all of us) are consumed with imposter syndrome, low self-esteem, or just plain embarrassment (or all three) at the idea of asking someone to buy our work. We get nervous about asking a friend to make that purchase: "Um, hey. I wrote something. Would you mind buying it? And maybe reading it? I mean, you don't have to, if you don't want to ... but would you?" If that's how we would feel about asking a friend, we can't even imagine asking a total stranger to do the same thing.

Listen, folks, you have a right to make money at this. Barring some sort of revolution or change in the way human beings think, we all expect to exchange goods or services for money. Stories – and the intellectual properties surrounding them – are goods that can and should be sold.

You busted your hump writing this grand tale. You spent your hard-earned cash on editing and a cover. You deserve to not just recoup your investment but to make a profit.

You got into this game because you love stories. They've ignited your imagination your whole life. The best tales live inside you forever – they made you happy or inspired or determined. And now, you've answered the calling that's been in your heart for as long as you can remember to do for others what your favorite authors did for you. That is noble. You were born an artist, and you're fulfilling your destiny by penning stories.

But being a starving artist is not living the dream. You don't have to suffer for your art, and you deserve to eat and have shelter and buy clothes for your family every bit as much as the doctor who takes care of your health, the teacher who educates your children, and the mechanic who fixes your car. Everyone deserves to be financially comfortable, including artists.

Stop being embarrassed to ask folks for money. They already expect to give it to you. You deserve it.

Likewise, asking people to buy is not sleazy. The authors who feel this way generally object to commercial enterprise in all its forms. They equate selling anything to unethically pushing products on people who don't need them. They view selling as tricking someone out of their money.

Selling someone your book isn't sleazy. You've crafted a well-written story designed to entertain and maybe educate. You deserve to be paid for that product.

A final objection to adding a CTA goes along the lines of: "Asking people to buy your book labels you as an indie, and people won't buy if they know that."

Let's go back to what I said about indie versus trad authors. First of all, most readers don't care whether books are self-published or not. They just want to read good stories mostly free of errors. They can get an indie book for $4.99, or a trad-house one for $10-15. Voracious readers know indie books are a good deal and happily buy them.

Second, it is possible to make a lot of money as an independently published author. But you cannot do it the way the trad houses do. You do not have the marketing budget, the deals with mega-bookstores, and the general name recognition to compete on the same stage as those published by the Big Five. Go to your local grocery store. In their tiny books and magazines section, are there any indie books there? I bet there are not. Indies don't have that kind of distribution available to them.

If you want to make the kind of money the big dogs in indie publishing are making, you have to level the playing field. You must do everything in your power to lower the barriers to sales.

And that means using the tried-and-true selling tactic of including a CTA.

So please, love yourself and your work enough to ask people to buy it. Put an effective CTA at the end of your blurb.

Being Clever

At Best Page Forward, our formula for the call to action goes like this:

> *Buy [BOOK TITLE] to [CLEVER PHRASE] today!*

The first half of the sentence should be pretty clear. We want them to buy, and we reiterate the title of the novel. Simple.

The end of the sentence is also straightforward. We want them to take action now. We don't want them to buy tomorrow, next week, or next year. We want them to buy it right now while we have them on the hook. That's why we always end with "today!"

But it's the clever phrase that requires some explanation. At BPF, we believe this helps set us (and by association our clients) apart in a crowded marketplace. Anyone can write something along the lines of, "Get your copy today!" That's a simple and effective CTA.

We want to do a little more. To do that, we add something a little special to spice it up. Here are some examples from films I've used previously in this book:

> *Buy* Toy Story *to travel to infinity and beyond today!*

Buy Superman: The Movie *to soar up, up and away today!*

Buy A Christmas Story *to unwrap hilarity today!*

In each of those, I took something directly related to the movie and made a cute, little turn of phrase out of it. For *Toy Story* and *Superman*, I used famous catchphrases for the heroes. For *A Christmas Story*, I made a reference to the idea of opening a present and then added "hilarity" to help convey the message that this film is a comedy.

The goal for each was to make it feel a little special. They give the reader an extra smile.

Just make sure that whatever you use ties to the book. You could write something like, "for a fantastic adventure today!" But that's not exactly unique to your novel. One could say that about stories as diverse as *20,000 Leagues Under the Sea*, *The Sandlot*, and *Thelma & Louise*. All of them could be called "fantastic adventures," but none of them is a thing like the others. Find something unique about your book that will make sense to a reader who is unfamiliar with the story.

Now, at Best Page Forward, we occasionally get pushback from authors who feel the clever phrase is "cheesy." I could rant about how treating puns and wordplay as cheesy is anti-intellectualism in action, but let's skip that.

Instead, think of it like this: Your job as an author is to manipulate language. In your book, you're stringing together sentences and paragraphs into pleasing, page-turning prose. With your blurb, you're attempting to write punchy, breezy copy that excites a reader and encourages them to buy.

Clever turns of phrase are not cheesy. They're not "groaners." They're you executing your craft to shape words to create effects. If a reader sees a clever phrase at the end of your blurb, their last impression will be that this book is well-written. Doesn't that sound like what you'd want readers to think?

Whether you choose to get clever at the end or not, though, you need a CTA. Tell the reader to buy your book. If they want to read your story, you deserve to be paid.

Homework

All right, this is it – the last step in your chosen books or movies you've been working with. Write a Call to Action for each one. Even if you plan to never use the clever-phrase portion of the BPF CTA formula, experiment with doing it here. It will help you practice your copywriting skills.

We've made it all the way through the basic formula for a well-written, compelling fiction blurb. But what if you've written a romance? What if you have a novel with two equally important protagonists?

In those cases, we need a 2-POV description. While they follow a similar formula, there are some key differences. Let's take a look at the 2-POV model in the next chapter.

If you're not in need of a 2-POV blurb, you can skip ahead to Chapter 19 for Memoir Blurbs, or Chapter 20 for advanced techniques.

CHAPTER 18
2-POV BLURBS

Sometimes, there is a second character important enough to warrant giving attention in the blurb. In romance in particular, we need more than a brief mention of this other person. They need to be developed as fully as our protagonist. In those cases, we alter the basic structure of the description to give them their own paragraph.

Now, if you're one of those people who skips ahead to the "good part," I've got a little bad news: This chapter covers the differences between a 1-POV and 2-POV blurb. If you went straight to this chapter, you'll need to back and read Chapter 9: The Gut Punch, Chapter 10: The Expansion, and Chapter 11: The Inciting Incident. Otherwise, the material here won't make much sense. Don't worry. I'll be here waiting for you if you need to go back.

A Note of Caution

If you're not writing a romance novel, it's unlikely you need this second point of view. There are exceptions but ask yourself if your book is really one of them. Spoiler alert: It probably isn't. The vast majority of non-romance novels are best treated with a 1-POV blurb.

Now listen, fantasy authors, I know you've written a grand epic about the fate of all existence with many important people playing their roles in the ultimate destiny of the realm. You do not have room for all these people in your blurb. One of them is the "most" main character, and that's the person you should be focused on.

You don't have space to give Aragorn his own paragraph, plus one for Merry and Pippin, and another for Legolas and Gimli. You will confuse your reader with all that detail, and they'll go look for something else to read that feels simpler.

Frodo Baggins is the main character of *The Lord of the Rings*. An entire epic may play out around him, but Frodo's quest to destroy The One Ring in Mt. Doom is the main plot of the story, and his journey with Sam and near-self-destruction are at the heart of the tale.

Your novel has a similar structure. There is a character around whom the story truly revolves. That's who you need to feature in your blurb. Whether you're writing a sci-fi/fantasy epic, a sweeping historical family saga, or a taut suspense novel, it's unlikely (though, I'll admit possible) that you need a second POV in your blurb to sell the book.

So, if you're not a romance writer, proceed through this chapter with caution.

No Bad Guys

Do not write a POV paragraph for your antagonist. Let me just repeat that for emphasis.

Do ***not*** *write a POV paragraph for your antagonist.*

If you've been paying close attention throughout, you should know why already. To sell your novel effectively, we need to create an emotional connection between your main character and the reader. They should want to root *for* the MC, not *against* them. No matter how sympathetic our villain's motivations may be, they are not the hero of the story. Therefore, they don't get a spot in the blurb.

That should also raise a question in your mind if you're considering a 2-POV blurb. How important is the emotional journey of this second character to the overall story? Does the main arc of the tale revolve around this character's inner journey in addition to the other MC's?

If you can't answer yes, then you don't need a second POV. If you answered yes, but the character in question is the antagonist, you don't need a second POV.

Even if your book is a tragedy, we should be rooting for the main character to succeed. We should want to see them on a journey that we hope will turn out all right.

And we shouldn't want that for the villain. From an actor's standpoint, the bad guy may be the most fun to play. But as the audience, we should not be rooting for them. We want to see the antagonist *fail* and the protagonist *succeed*.

So, no bad guys in the blurb, except as obstacles to the hero.

The 2-POV Structure

As a reminder, the template for a blurb with two points of view is:

The Hook

P1S1: *The Gut Punch*

P1S2: *The Expansion*

P1S3: *The Inciting Incident*

P2S1: *The Uppercut*

P2S2: *The Inciting Incident (Again)*

P2S3: *The Consequence*

P3S1: *The First Complication*

P3S2: *The Second Complication*

The Cliffhanger

The Selling Paragraph

The Call to Action

Much of this is exactly the same as what we've already seen. The hook, all of P1, the cliffhanger, the selling paragraph, and the call to action are just like what we'd find in the standard template.

It's when we get to P2 and P3 that things are a little different. Let's go over each of those new sentences in detail.

The Uppercut

In P1, we had the gut punch – a short, impactful sentence of six to ten words to grab the reader's full attention. In any type of martial arts, the first blow is a setup for a devastating follow. Hitting someone in the stomach causes someone to double over, which makes it easier to hit them in the jaw with that massive uppercut.

That's what we're doing with our P2S1. We're going to deliver another six-to-ten-word shot to the jaw, introducing the initial emotional state of our MC2. Just like we did with MC1, we want to grab the reader's full attention.

For example, let's say we were writing a blurb for *Casablanca*. Our P1 might go something like:

> *Rick Blaine put the past firmly behind him. Running a café and casino in Vichy-controlled Morocco, the former mercenary keeps his business strictly neutral and his heart under lock and key. But when the woman who betrayed him shows up in his bar desperate for help, old feelings flood back in and threaten his well-honed aloof attitude.*

We've got our eight-word gut punch introducing Rick. Our expansion is next, wherein we detail his situation and his emotional state. The inciting incident is Ilse showing up at the café and bringing back all his old memories.

Now that we've established that, we can introduce Ilse, our MC2, with the uppercut:

> *Ilsa Lund will do anything to escape the Nazis.*

Once again, we've gone nice and short, with only nine words. We've hit hard by immediately outlining her desperation – she would do anything to escape the Nazis.

It's important to deliver an equally devastating punch with our P2S1. We've just switched points of view and introduced a new character. That can be jarring and lead to some confusion. We counter that by hammering the reader with another compelling emotional conflict.

We already know we're in Vichy-controlled Morocco, which means World War II is in full swing. Germany is at the height of its power at this time, marching across the continent and dispatching nearly every foe in her way. Fleeing the Nazis is a very real worry for a lot of people and putting our heroine at risk of capture immediately allows us to feel her fear and desperation.

Remember that each sentence in your blurb needs to raise the stakes from the previous one. While we're starting over with a new POV, we still need to build on what we've already established. By opening with Ilse fleeing the Nazis, that raises the stakes on Rick's practiced neutrality in one of the few sanctuaries from the war.

The Inciting Incident (Again)

Before we dive fully into P2S2, let's discuss the inciting incident from P1S3. In a romance, the inciting incident is always the meet-cute.

The structure of any romance is a story about two people meeting, falling in love, overcoming obstacles, and living happily ever after. Therefore, the inciting incident – the external event that forces the MC out of their current situation and into the action of the narrative – has to be the moment the two lovers meet.

(To be fair, *Casablanca* breaks a lot of the romance rules, but as one of film history's greatest love stories, it remains a good model for blurb writing.)

So, if we go back to P1S3, we ended with MC1 meeting MC2. We can see this in our example from above:

> *But when the woman who betrayed him shows up in his bar desperate for help, old feelings flood back in and threaten his well-honed aloof attitude.*

Ilse shows up at Rick's Café Americain and asks Sam to play "As Time Goes By." Rick storms out of his office upon hearing it, and ... he sees her.

Boom. Everything changes immediately. Every feeling and emotion he's repressed since fleeing Paris ahead of the Nazi conquest comes flooding back. Try as he might to resist, he's immediately back in love with her.

That's the event that propels the rest of the story forward. Will he help Ilse and her Resistance-leader husband get out of Casablanca? Will he allow his anger to consume him and let them fend for themselves? Will Ilse forsake her husband for her true love, Rick? Or will she leave our hero bitter and broken again?

The plot of the film revolves around these questions. That makes their meeting in the café the inciting incident.

Now, in a two-person blurb, we don't want to simply mirror the structure of P1. First, parallel construction will bore the reader. They'll be able to recognize that P2 is exactly like P1, which will feel stagnant and therefore dull.

Frankly, we want to move the story forward. If both paragraphs end on the inciting incident, then nothing has really happened. We spent three sentences setting up the story. We then used the next three sentences to do it again. After six sentences and two paragraphs, we're no closer to finding out what happens after the inciting incident.

However, we still need it in P2, particularly in romance, where the meet-cute drives the two characters together. Instead of waiting until P2S3, we're going to reintroduce the inciting incident from MC2's perspective right after the uppercut.

Continuing with our example:

> *But when she and her husband arrive in Casablanca, she never expected to run into the one man she truly loved.*

Ilse and her husband come to Casablanca because it's the route to get to Lisbon, and eventually the United States. But she doesn't know until they arrive, that Rick is there, too. Although she's devoted to her husband, Rick is the man she's in love with.

So, we have our inciting incident from Ilse's perspective, and we've raised the stakes from the first time we saw it in P1S3. P2S2 is the first we hear of her husband, so that immediately complicates the romance. And we discover Rick is the "one man she truly loved." The tension is definitely building here!

The Consequence

Since we just reiterated the inciting incident, we've got to jack the stakes up further. Because just like in P1S3, we want to end with a cliffhanger. Once again, we need to push the reader into the next paragraph. We therefore want things to be just as exciting for MC2 as they were for MC1.

I call this sentence the consequence, because typically what we're going to do here is discuss what it would mean if MC2 allowed themselves to get involved with MC1. We're going to either give the emotional consequences of falling for this person, or the potential story consequences of choosing one path or the other.

For example:

> *And when it turns out he holds the key to freedom, she feels the passion they once shared reignite.*

We've got major consequences here. She's married. She and her husband are trying to escape to Portugal. But all that passion she felt with Rick has suddenly reignited. That's kind of a problem for her.

But it gets stickier, because what truly brings all that flooding back is that Rick has the means to give her exactly what she needs – passage from Casablanca for her heroic husband. So, what does she do? Can she convince Rick to help? Will there be a price? And what about her heart?

We've got some major potential consequences here. Wanting to know what might happen drives us into the next paragraph to find out.

The First Complication

You'll recall in the standard blurb template, P2S2 is the complication. In a 2-POV description, not only have we got more than one obstacle for the protag, they're in a different place.

The third paragraph is only two sentences long (just as P2 was in the standard blurb). Each of those sentences features one of the main characters. The basic outline of P3S1 goes like this:

> *MC1 is falling for MC2, but there's a complication that could keep them apart.*

If you're not writing a romance, then the first complication is a little more plot-oriented. But with romance, it's all about what could interfere with the happy ending.

> *Falling for her all over again, Rick fights the urge to rekindle the affair with the gorgeous married woman.*

So, Rick can't resist her. But he must because she's married. He's struggling against his urge to hold her in his arms again.

If we wanted, we could make this more about the papers to get out of Casablanca:

> *Knowing it would be easy to give her the papers she needs to get her to freedom, Rick despairs of losing the gorgeous woman all over again.*

This gives him a different kind of a conflict. He knows he could do the right thing to help her. But the emotional cost to him would be heavy. Once again, we have a plot complication that could keep them from getting together, which raises the emotional stakes.

The Second Complication

Our P3S2 follows this format:

> *MC2 is falling for MC1, but there's ANOTHER complication that could keep them apart.*

While the structure is nearly identical to P3S1, there are a couple of differences we need to make note of. First, we've switched POV's. Because we gave MC2 their own POV paragraph, we need to give them a sentence from their perspective in P3. Otherwise, there would be no reason for them to have their own paragraph. We'd just keep everything in MC1's head and shorten this whole thing down.

To make this work, we need to have MC2's name as close to the front of the sentence as possible. If we wait too long, it can be confusing to the reader as to whose mind we're in.

Second, the second complication must be different from the first complication. If both characters have the same obstacle, we're essentially treading water, not really going anywhere. That doesn't raise the stakes, which can cause the reader to lose interest.

Speaking of which, not only must the second complication be different from the first, it must raise the stakes from wherever the first complication left us. Things have to keep getting more dramatic.

So, for example:

> *And though Ilse knows her loyalty should be to her spouse, she is torn between her duty and her desire.*

That puts Ilse at the front of the sentence, so we know we're inside her perspective. It sorta raises the stakes from where we left Rick. But it really just restates the same conflict Rick is having: They want to be together, but she's married to an important man. What if we tweaked it to read thus:

> *And though Ilse knows her loyalty should be to her spouse, she is torn between her duty to help continue the Resistance and the desire burning in her heart.*

Now, we've got some major stakes. We're not just talking about leaving her husband. She could be letting down the whole revolution. That's kind of a big deal. But the choice is giving up her heart's desire – the one man she truly loves. That takes these global stakes and makes them intensely personal.

Then, if we combine it with our second version of Rick's sentence, we'd have:

> *Knowing it would be easy to give her the papers she needs to get her to freedom, Rick despairs of losing the gorgeous woman all over again. And though Ilse knows her loyalty should be to her spouse, she is torn between her duty to help continue the Resistance and the desire burning in her heart.*

So, Rick's got the papers, but can he bear to lose her? Ilse knows she should stay with her husband to fight the good fight instead of leaving with Rick. But that would break her heart. That's all the tension we need to drive readers into the cliffhanger and make them want to know what happens.

Homework

Romance authors, this is your moment. I'm betting at least one of those books or films you chose was actually a romance. Throw out your P2 and craft a proper 2-POV blurb for it.

If you didn't choose a romance for any of your exercises, take a look at your choices. Is there one where there's a strong secondary character you could use? If not, here are a few examples you could pick for this exercise that have two main characters but are not romance:

- *Toy Story* (Woody and Buzz)
- *Frozen* (Anna and Elsa)
- *Lethal Weapon* (Riggs and Murtaugh)
- *Bill & Ted's Excellent Adventure* (Bill and Ted)
- *Gilmore Girls* (Lorelei and Rory)

You can probably think of a few others if you don't like any of those or are unfamiliar with all of them. The point is, select a story that has two driving characters and give them each a POV paragraph and then a P3 with two complications.

There's one more template to share with you. If you're a memoir writer, the next chapter is for you. If you're not, you can skip ahead to Chapter 20 for advanced techniques.

CHAPTER 19
MEMOIRS

Of all the books to write blurbs for, memoirs are the trickiest. Technically, they're nonfiction books. However, they're told in narrative fashion like a novel. So, what's the right approach?

At Best Page Forward, we treat memoirs like fiction. Sort of. We follow most of the conventions for the standard fiction blurb template, just as I've outlined here over the last several chapters. But there are some key differences to crafting a compelling description for this unique form of storytelling.

Go to the Past

As we mentioned all the way back in Chapter 8, book blurbs are written in present tense. But a memoir recounts true events that have already happened. So, this is the one exception to our rule. We use past tense to describe the events, both in the hook and in the body. This helps signify the book is a recounting of previous experiences.

Let's pretend *Hamilton* is a memoir instead of a biography. Our hook might read something like:

He came to New York to make a name for himself. He never imagined he would help found a nation.

We're in past tense here – "he *came* to New York...." "He never *imagined*...."

Likewise, we might do something of this nature for our opening:

Alexander Hamilton was not throwin' away his shot.

Once again, we're setting this clearly in the past – "was not" instead of "is not throwin' away." This helps us establish the memoir format.

One or Two Paragraphs for the Narrative

Depending on how much material you want to include, you can either go with one or two paragraphs for the body of the blurb. However, they still follow the same format:

P1S1: *The Gut Punch*

P1S2: *The Expansion*

P1S3: *The Inciting Incident*

P2S1: *The Bridge*

P2S2: *The Complication*

Essentially, P2 is optional. You'll have the gut punch, the expansion, and the inciting incident regardless, and then you can decide if you want the bridge and the complication.

Now, you may be thinking, "Wait a second, Phoebe, this is nonfiction. There's no inciting incident to the story."

But let's remember that this is *narrative* nonfiction. It's written as though it were a story. And what's the definition of the inciting incident? An external event that forces the main character out of their initial state and into the action.

In the case of a memoir, our main character is the author. The inciting incident is the thing that forces the person into the extraordinary account of their life they have to share.

For example, *Marley & Me* is a memoir about a *lot* of things. But the frame of the story is John Grogan getting a yellow lab puppy without knowing a thing about how to take care of dogs, especially high-energy breeds like Labradors. The inciting incident is Grogan and his wife bringing home the titular canid.

Is your memoir about coming to America and struggling to fit in? We've got several possibilities depending on the nature of the story. It could be whatever force in your home country has made you expatriate. It could be landing on U.S. soil and immediately being overwhelmed by the cultural differences. It could be showing up at school or work, eager to get started, only to face bigotry or rules or regulations that make it hard.

Looking at *A Christmas Story*, which is loosely based on Jean Shepherd's childhood, the inciting incident is the moment Ralphie's mother tells him he can't have a BB-gun because he'll shoot his eye out.

Just like in fiction, there is an external force that pushes our author from whatever situation they were in at the start of the book into the sequence of events that follows.

The Cliffhanger

This is another piece of the standard blurb template that is optional. At Best Page Forward, we use it sometimes and other times not. It sort of depends on what we've included so far. Sometimes, asking a "will they or won't they" question doesn't make sense, because we're going to answer it in the next paragraph (see below).

As a general rule, if you only go with one paragraph of fiction-style blurb, a cliffhanger makes a lot of sense. We don't want to leave the readers feeling like they don't know enough to make a decision. If you have two paragraphs, then the cliff is a little easier to let go.

We can have our cliffhanger follow the standard fiction format by asking a question about whether the author will succeed. Returning to *Hamilton*, we could do something like:

> *Would Hamilton at last succeed in crafting a constitution that built a firm foundation for the future?*

That's got that sort of will-he-or-won't-he feel to it. Just like with fiction, we ask if our author can conquer the foes in front of them.

But another way to do it that often works better for memoir looks like this:

> *But he would discover that winning a revolution against the most-powerful empire in the world was easy compared to building a country.*

Here, we've gone to a statement format that leaves us wondering what will happen. Winning the American Revolution wasn't the hard part? Oh, my! What's next?

A lot of times at Best Page Forward, we'll open the cliffhanger with, "But their greatest challenge yet would be ..." This allows us to accomplish the same thing. We make people wonder if the author will be able to get around this next, bigger obstacle.

Switching Gears

Up until this point, we've been acting as though this were a novel. But as I noted at the top of the chapter, it isn't fiction, and our readers need to understand that to avoid any confusion. Now, we're going to shift our approach to nonfiction. At Best Page Forward, we call this the "explainer paragraph," and like every other blurb type, it has its own template.

P3S1: *The Explanation*

P3S2: *The Story*

P3S3: *The Benefit*

Let's look at each sentence in depth.

The Explanation

This is where we're going to tell the reader that this is actually a memoir. We try to avoid using that specific word, so that we can have it for the selling paragraph when we're describing genre, but this sentence amounts to us saying, "Hey, this book is a memoir."

Let's return to *Marley & Me*, since it actually *is* a memoir. If we were writing a blurb for it, the explanation might look something like this:

> Marley & Me: Life and Love with the World's Worst Dog *is a hilarious and heart-wrenching journey through one man's deep friendship with a canine criminal.*

We shared our title, plus we've told the reader some key things about it. A "hilarious and heart-wrenching journey" tells us this is a memoir and that it covers a broad spectrum of emotions. What's it about? A man and his dog. Everything the reader needs to know is right there.

The Story

Having explained that this is a memoir, we now need to tell the reader a little more about how the information is presented. They sort of know this already, since it's a memoir. But this is our opportunity to dig into the particulars of what's inside.

> *With self-deprecating wit and sweet sincerity, Grogan chronicles the madcap misadventures of a 97-pound behemoth who ate furniture, drooled on guests, and was expelled from obedience school.*

Several things are going on here. First, we're telling the reader about the tone of the book. Our author is sweet and sincere. He also employs self-deprecating wit to poke fun at the mistakes he makes. This tells us the book will be both funny and sentimental.

It also tells us some of the events we're going to encounter. The dog eats furniture! He was *expelled* from obedience school! That's going to interest anyone looking for a funny memoir about a dog.

Finally, we've raised the stakes from P3S1. There, we described the book as a hilarious and heart-wrenching journey of life with a canine criminal. Now that we know some of the specifics, the stakes have gone up even higher.

All of this combines to draw the reader deeper into the story, making them want to know what happens to our author and his dog.

The Benefit

While some memoirs are generally entertaining yarns about the author's life, most of them have something they want to say. The person isn't telling their story just so someone will read about them. Rather, they have something they want to accomplish. They are sharing their story so others can benefit from it.

The final sentence in the explanation paragraph turns the book outward. We describe what a person will get out of reading it. Continuing with our example:

> *And as they struggle to cope with the havoc Marley wreaks on their lives, his loyalty and selfless love for the family teaches everyone the importance of accepting each other as they are.*

Here, we make it clear that living with this dog is a struggle. But the animal's devotion to everyone in the family unit provides an important life lesson. That is an inspiring idea. We'll get the humor of the dog's antics but also the implication that the reader is going to come away from this book feeling awed.

. . .

The Selling Paragraph

The SP is largely the same as with the standard template. But our first sentence doubles down on where we left things at the end of P3S3. For instance:

> Marley & Me *is an emotional memoir about the triumphs and pitfalls of building a family.*

Here, we've mentioned this is a memoir, and we've used an adjective to describe it – "emotional." We chose that tone, because the book features some dark emotions and personal tragedies along with the hijinks. If the book had been just about the dog's shenanigan's we might have gone a little more lighthearted. But Grogan's book covers a lot of ground, so I wanted to make sure that came across.

Next, your SPS2 will run just like the other templates:

> *If you like X, Y, and Z, then you'll love [AUTHOR NAME]'s [ADJECTIVE] account/story/tale/etc.*

To summarize, we approach memoirs like fiction but write the synopsis in past tense to convey that these things have already happened. Then, we add a nonfiction "explainer paragraph" so that it's clear this is a memoir that will address a particular subject. All that helps us fit comfortably into the vague, in-between space of not-fiction and not-exactly-nonfiction.

Homework

Pick your favorite memoir. Try writing a blurb for it. Remember that it needs to contain all the elements a fiction description does – especially an inciting incident. Add the explanation paragraph to capture the feel of the book, so the reader has a clear idea what they'll be getting.

Whew! That's it! We've finally gotten through the structure of a good blurb. Next up, we'll look at the advanced tactics that will really round your description into compelling ad copy.

Ready? Then turn the page, and let's get started!

CHAPTER 20

TONE AND TECHNIQUE

It's time to make things shine. We're in the spit-and-polish phase, where we shape the language to make folks want to buy. This chapter will teach you the finer points of excellent ad copy.

Multiple Drafts

You'll probably hate hearing this, but you need to write multiple drafts of your blurb. Just as you wouldn't publish the first draft of your novel, you'll want to edit and shape your description to make it really sing. Copywriting is both an art and a science, and like all writing, it needs polishing.

At Best Page Forward, our process looks like this:

- Blurb is assigned to a first draft writer, who reads the submission, researches the book, and then pens a proposed draft
- Approval editor reads the pitch and the submission, makes sure everything looks right, and orders any changes

- First draft writer writes the blurb, incorporating the approval editor's suggestions
- Final drafter takes the first draft and makes changes, tightening phrases, cleaning up language, and generally shaping the blurb into the form the customer will ultimately see
- Final draft reviewer fact-checks, tunes the language further, and looks for other opportunities to improve the copy
- Bryan's reviewer (named for our fearless leader, who used to do this stage solely himself) tightens down the last few screws, making sure it is the absolute best work we can do before we send it on to the customer for approval

That's six steps, comprising five drafts of the blurb. Sometimes, the finished product looks a lot like the first drafter's initial pitch. Sometimes, it's very different. But the goal is to make sure we've really refined the description into punchy, effective copy.

Now, you may be thinking, "Uh, I don't have four other people to help me work on this, Phoebs. It's just me working on this."

That's totally okay. You can do this all yourself. My point in illustrating the BPF process is to show you there are multiple drafts from assignment to final delivery.

A lot of the magic happens at the final-draft stage. And it's not because our editors are amazing (although, they are). It's due to what the first drafters give them to work with. A Best Page Forward first draft has the following required elements:

- Hook
- **Three** options for the gut punch
- The expansion
- **Three** options for the inciting incident
- **Two** options for the bridge
- The complication
- **Three** options for the cliffhanger
- Selling paragraph
- **Three** options for the CTA

- **Five** alternate hooks for Amazon ad copy

Notice how many sentences in the draft require multiple iterations? We do this because we know that the first idea isn't always the best one. Our editors frequently *combine* options. They might take the front half of one sentence and marry it to the back half of another. They might decide one of those Amazon ad copy lines is a better headline for the blurb and swap it out.

The point is, we don't sit down and write a blurb from stem to stern in a single pass. We put a whole bunch of options on the table, so we can pick out the very best for an outstanding description. You should do the same.

Tone

When we advertise anything, we want to give the potential buyer a taste of what they'll be getting. You wouldn't adopt a comedic voice if you were pitching a story like *The Silence of the Lambs*, and treating *Bill & Ted's Excellent Adventure* like it's *All the President's Men* would be a fatal mistake. Why? Because you'll set the wrong expectations for the story's content. The wrong people will show up, and you'll get bad reactions. People won't finish it, and they may decide to give it a one-star review.

One of the truisms I've observed in life is that nothing infuriates people more than unmet expectations. Politicians who promise prosperity and then crash the economy tend to lose elections. Restaurants that promise five-star service and then deliver awful food end up going out of business. Likewise, books that promise one sort of reading experience and then deliver another get bad reviews and poor sales.

The tone of your blurb is essential in helping bring the right readers to your fiction. Understand this right now: Not everyone out there is going to like your book. No matter how well-plotted or well-written it is, there are folks who won't dig the kinds of things you write. If you pen space opera with magic-driven technology, fans of hard science fiction are going to hate it. If you author feminist literary fiction with deep human themes and slow-burn romance, you'll have a difficult time finding purchase with readers of cold-hearted vigilante thrillers.

This is okay. I'd even go so far as to say it's great. Why? Because there are plenty of people who will *love* your books. Cater to them and let the folks who think your novel is trash read the stories that appeal to them. Everyone wins that way.

Tone is the tool you use to make sure the right readers buy and the wrong readers do not.

Genre Markers

At Best Page Forward, one of our techniques is to deliberately use words in the description that are frequently associated with the genre in question. These marker words signal to the reader not only the genre of the book, but its subcategory too.

For example, fantasy has several different subgenres, and they each have a peculiar tone to them. Noblebright fantasy, while it can have some dark moments, has an overall hopeful outlook. We therefore want to choose words that convey this sense of optimism that the world can indeed be saved from evil. In the selling paragraph, we might describe such a story as "uplifting" or "inspiring." Our characters would have traits such as "noble," "dedicated," "loyal," etc. These all convey that good-conquers-all philosophy that permeates the story.

By way of contrast, grimdark fantasy sees the world as doomed. The forces of evil are everywhere, and they can never be fully defeated. Indeed, the best we can hope for is justice, which often takes a violent and bloody form. Where noblebright fantasy might have a Chosen One trope, the hero generally must work with others to vanquish the bad guy. Grimdark, on the other hand, typically features a lone warrior fighting a vain battle against darkness with little help from anyone else. To convey that, we want to use words like "grim," "dark," "bloody," "gory," "impossible," etc. These all tell us this is not going to be a sunny, happy tale.

Urban fantasy often features a sarcastic narrator, who copes with their situation with gallows humor and cutting remarks. That type of book requires us to make sure the snark comes through in the ad copy. Words like, "strong," "sarcastic," "snarky," "clever," "world-weary," etc. tell the reader that they can expect an MC whose tongue is as sharp as their sword.

Genre markers alert readers to the things they're looking for in an engaging read. Here are some more examples:

- *Children's Literature:* Charming, Endearing, Fun, Lighthearted, Sweet, Tender
- *Comedy:* Charming, Farce/Farcical, Hilarious/Hilarity, Humor/Humorous, Laugh-out-loud, Outrageous, Satire/Satirical, Sidesplitting
- *Coming-of-Age:* Beautiful, Inspirational/Inspiring, Timeless, Universal, Young
- *Crime:* Betrayal, Bloody, Dark, Calculating, Duplicitous, Grim, Gritty, Noir, Vicious
- *Family Saga:* Bold/Boldly, Clan, Expansive, Epic, Family, Intimate, Sweeping
- *Fantasy:* Dark/Darkness, Dragon, Enchanting, Epic, Mage/Magic, Sinister, Sorcerer/Sorcery, Sword, Warrior, Wizard
- *Historical:* Detail/Detailed, Historic, Period, Research/Researched, Rich/Richly, Time
- *Horror:* Creepy, Dark/Darkness, Evil, Fear/Fearful, Horrific, Monstrous, Nightmare/Nightmarish, Terror/Terrifying, Unspeakable
- *Literary Fiction:* Bold, Engaging, Human Spirit, Insightful, Timeless, Triumph Universal
- *Mystery, Cozy:* Charming, Clever, Endearing, Hilarious, Killer, Light, Murder/Murderer, Sharp, Whodunit
- *Mystery, Dark:* Blood-soaked/Bloody, Grim, Gritty, Killer, Madman, Murderer/Murderer, Noir, Sadistic, Vicious

- *Post-Apocalyptic:* All that's left/Left behind, Apocalypse, Armageddon, Dark, Grim, Hostile, Ruin, Survive/Survival, Undead, Zombie
- *Romance, Clean & Wholesome:* Falling For, Forever, Gorgeous, Handsome, Happily Ever After, Head-over-heels, Heart's Desire, Innocent, Sweet, Tender, Wholesome
- *Romance, Medium Heat:* Desire, Determined, Enraptured, Loving, Gorgeous, Handsome, Hunk/Hunky, Sexy, Strong
- *Romance, Steamy/Erotica:* Bedroom, Control, Desire, Hot/Red-hot/White-hot, Passion/Passionate, Scorching, Sexy, Strong, Sultry
- *Sci-Fi, Alien Invasion:* Alien, Annihilation, Attack/Attacking, Conquer/Conquering/Conquest, Extinction, Extra-terrestrial, Fleet/Armada, Invasion, Occupation
- *Sci-Fi, Cyberpunk:* AI/Artificial Intelligence, Computer, Cyber/Cyborg, Gear, Hack/Hacker, Hardwire, Interface, Tech/Technology, Wet-tech
- *Sci-Fi, Genetic Engineering:* Breakthrough, DNA, Experiment/Experimental, Gene/Gene-splicing/Genetic, Lab/Laboratory, Science/Scientist
- *Sci-Fi, Military/Space Opera:* AI/Artificial Intelligence, Alien, Attack, Captain, FTL, Hyperdrive/Hyperspace, Planet, Space, Starship
- *Superhero:* Abilities, Fiendish, Heroic, Master Plan, Powerful/Powers, Sinister, Superhuman/Metahuman/Inhuman
- *Suspense:* Atmospheric, Brooding, Creepy, Foreboding, Hair-raising, Haunted/Haunting, Nail-biting, Page-turning, Stalker/Stalking, Terrifying
- *Thriller, Conspiracy:* Cabal, Conspiracy, Far-reaching, Isolated, Network, On the Run, Organization, Secret, Sinister, Vast
- *Thriller, Espionage:* Action-packed, Agency/Agent, Assignment, Code, High-octane, Intel/Intelligence, Mission, Sniper, Spook, Spy, Target, Page-turning

- *Thriller, Religious/Archaeology:* Ancient, Apocalypse/Apocalyptic, Biblical, Fast-paced, Forgotten, Hidden, Lost, Pulse-pounding, Tomb, Well-researched
- *Western:* Corrupt/Corruption, Cowboy, Desperado, Dusty, Horse, Honor, Ranch/Rancher, Rider, Six-gun/Six-shooter, Stranger, Thrilling
- *Young Adult:* Bully, Captivating, Desperate, Determined, Fiery, Gripping, Lost, Nobody, Outspoken, Teen/Teenaged/Teenager, Understand/Understanding, Young

As usual, that list is by no means exhaustive, but it should give you a place to get started.

Alliteration

If you're not familiar with the term, alliteration is the practice of stringing together several words with similar sounds. For example:

> Fantastic Fiction Blurbs *is a fascinating frolic in the fields of fine copywriting.*

We've got a *lot* of "f" sounds in there. Not only are there two in the title, but we have four more in the rest of the sentence. They also all occur in close proximity to one another. This helps create a pleasing, poetic sound to the sentence.

Alliteration works well to convey a light and even comical tone. It's a frequent and effective tactic in cozy mystery, humor, children's books, and even poetry blurbs. It feels fun and clever. You wouldn't use it for grimdark fantasy or gritty serial-killer thrillers, but if you need to keep the mood light in your description, alliteration goes a long way towards making that happen.

Puns and Wordplay

Another favorite of the cozy-mystery genre, this tactic can really help you drive home tone and genre. Essentially, you engage in a play on words' typical meanings to nudge the reader in the ribs.

For example, if we were writing a blurb for *Bull Durham*, we might like to use baseball metaphors to convey the humor prevalent throughout the film. Our hook might look something this:

> *She believes in the Church of Baseball. He's desperate to make it to The Show. When they meet at the ballpark, will love step up to the plate?*

The final phrase establishes a lot. We can tell it's a romance because we're asking if love will step up. And by using the baseball metaphor of "step up to the plate," we know this is a sports romance that likely is comedic in tone, since there's a pun.

Wordplay doesn't have to indicate comedy, though. A blurb's job, you'll recall, is to sell the book. Clever, catchy copy helps engage the reader's mind. We could use it effectively for a story as chilling as *The Silence of the Lambs*. What if our cliffhanger was something like:

> *Can Claire follow the trail to a madman without becoming the next woman in the morgue?*

Being the next in the morgue is a play on words. It's clever without losing the seriousness. Since Buffalo Bob removes his victim's skin, we could also do something like:

> *Can Claire catch a killer without losing her skin?*

The wordplay is there to tickle the reader's mind, but we've done it in a way to increase the sense of horror rather than invoke humor.

Whatever some people will tell you about punning being "cheesy," the human mind likes it. Recognizing that cleverness with the language creates a dopamine hit in the brain that feels good. Most importantly, making someone feel nice when they are reading your description helps you get the sale.

Bathos

This is a comedy technique that works best with hooks, although you can use it effectively throughout your blurb if you're good at it. Bathos lowers the stakes, often to the mundane, to get a laugh. To make it work, you have to build things up really high, and then drop them off a cliff so it reads as ridiculous.

My all-time favorite example of bathos is the tagline for the movie, *Army of Darkness:*

> *Lost in time. Surrounded by evil. Low on gas.*

The genius of the line lies in the stakes. The writer builds them carefully to a major height before pushing them over a cliff. Being lost in time sounds bad. Being lost anywhere is generally not good, but lost in time? That sounds even worse. Then, in addition to being lost in time, our protagonist is surrounded by evil. That's taken the stakes to a whole new level. Being surrounded by evil is *always* bad (unless you're the villain). Having it come after establishing that our hero is also lost in time, makes the situation direr.

Then we hit the punchline: Low on gas. Being low on gas isn't exactly good, but when we compare it to being lost in time or surrounded by evil, it's a walk in the park. By putting it at end of the hook, it turns the whole thing funny.

Another fine use of bathos is in the tagline for *Bill & Ted's Excellent Adventure:*

> *History is about to be rewritten by two guys who can't spell....*

Rewriting history is huge. But the implication is the guys about to do so don't know the first thing about it. Rightly or wrongly, being unable to spell well is seen as a mark of lower intelligence. Setting up the enormous stakes of rewriting history and then suggesting the people about to do it are going to make a mess of everything gives it a funny tone.

That tagline is also a fine example of wordplay (see above). "Rewritten" invokes the image of someone penning the history of the world, paired with "can't spell." Since spelling is a key component of writing, this clever pun paints a picture of a couple of dummies trying to write the history of the world, maybe with a crayon.

The combination of bathos and punning make this a well-constructed piece of copy that perfectly conveys the tone of the movie.

Trading Down Words

Less is often more with ad copy. At Best Page Forward, we're always looking to axe unnecessary words from the blurb. We call this technique "trading down words," and the principle is fairly simple. Can we turn ten words into seven? Can we make seven words into five? What about four?

Let's go back to that Essential Elements chapter. The very first key ingredient to a good blurb that I mentioned was brevity. Once again, we live in the age of distractions and low attention spans. So, book descriptions need to be fast and punchy. Short, smooth sentences are critical to holding reader interest.

For example, suppose we had a description for a thriller in which unlocking a secret code was absolutely essential to thwarting the villain. We might have something like:

If he doesn't figure out the code in time, the world may be doomed.

That's fairly simple and direct. We have clear stakes in a short sentence that allows the reader to feel the danger of the ticking clock. But what if we traded down some words:

If he can't crack the code, the world is doomed.

Notice how much stronger that is? We've gone from fourteen words to ten. It's shorter and more direct. We've done it by using more powerful words. In our first version, the hero had to "figure out" the code. In the second version, he has to "crack" it. Not only is that one word instead of two, it's one syllable instead of three. That makes it hit harder. Also, "crack" has that good, powerful, hard-C sound at both the beginning and the end. That adds impact as well.

We've also increased the stakes. We went from the world "may be doomed" to "*is* doomed." That took us from two words to one and from six characters to two, both of which help speed up the sentence. But we also removed doubt and replaced it with certainty. Our hero has to crack this code, or everyone is going to die. No question about it. That really jacks up the stakes.

Finally, by cutting "in time," we've streamlined the sentence. On the one hand, it removes the ticking clock, which could lower the stakes. But we've made it imperative to crack the code, because the world is destined for destruction if he fails. In this case, that added concept of the countdown isn't necessary to kick the stakes up to the highest level. Therefore, removing it improves the sentence.

Clichés

If you've studied writing at any level, you've no doubt been told to avoid clichés. "It's lazy writing," you've likely been admonished. "It doesn't show any degree of craft."

Hopefully, one of the most important lessons you've taken away from this book is the idea that copywriting and prose are two entirely different animals. (See what I did there?) Yes, you absolutely should avoid clichés in your fiction.

But they're perfectly acceptable in your blurb.

I'll remind you again that the purpose of a book description is to *sell* the book. And using clichéd phrases helps you accomplish that. There are several reasons why.

First, and most importantly, you need to keep the reader engaged in your copy. The more they have to think about what the words mean, the less they are enchanted by the tale you're spinning. A cliché is a shorthand way to get meaning across. It's easily recognizable.

If I describe a character as "a fish out of water," readers immediately know what that means. I don't have to tell them that bookworm Janet has no idea how to navigate being in the social spotlight organizing the school dance. "Fish out of water" does all that for me in four words. It works just as well to describe Clark's first day at a major metropolitan newspaper after having grown up on a farm in Western Kansas.

Second, just like with clever wordplay, it provides a dopamine hit in the brain. We haven't discussed a lot about brain chemistry and the power of hormones. But dopamine is released when you recognize something. That sense of familiarity makes us feel good. It's comforting. Seeing a turn of phrase that we recognize immediately and understand creates positive feelings in the mind. Once again, creating that sense of happiness when a reader looks at your blurb predisposes them towards wanting to buy.

Now, you shouldn't layer on the clichés like frosting on a cake. Too much of a good thing is bad. If every sentence has one, you'll create irritation that makes the reader believe the writing inside the book is as lazy as the copy describing it. But a few clichés here and there work in your favor. Don't avoid them like the plague.

Echoes (Echoes, Echoes, Echoes ...)

This is one of those techniques that really separates the pros from the amateurs. Closely repeated words – what we call, "echoes," at Best Page Forward – grate on the reader's mind. Now, utility words like articles, prepositions, and conjunctions generally don't cause this effect.

(Although if every sentence begins with "But," you will irritate your potential customer.)

It's nouns and verbs where this really has an effect. If we were writing a blurb for, say, *On Golden Pond*, we can only use "fish" or "fishing" one time. Do it twice, and the reader notices. Do it three time or more, and they start tuning out.

Echoes really work against smooth, effective copy. They can be harder to eliminate than you think. Synonyms are a good way to get around them. A thesaurus is a tool every writer should have at their fingertips.

But you have to be careful. Not all synonyms are a good fit. For example, a word like "psychology" doesn't have a lot of *good* synonyms. Maybe "behaviorism" works okay. But then, will that word fit neatly into your ad copy? Probably not. Words like this should be used once and then avoided.

As good a solution for echoes as synonyms are, sometimes it's best to rewrite the sentence in such a way that you don't need the word. Let's say we had established our MC as an expert in criminal psychology. We wouldn't want to say something like:

> *Studying the psychology of the killer, Jenkins follows the clues to an abandoned warehouse.*

Since we presumably used "psychology" in a previous sentence, repeating it is glaring. And subbing in a word like "behavior" or "mindset" doesn't feel as strong. But what if we rewrote the sentence to read:

> *Trying to put himself in the killer's head, Jenkins follows the clues to an abandoned warehouse.*

Now, we've got that same idea, but we did it in a way that neither "psychology" nor a synonym for it was necessary.

This principle applies to variations on a word, too. If you call your antagonist, "the killer," you can't use "kill," "killed," or "killing" elsewhere in the blurb. They're all too similar. You need a synonym like, "murder," "murdered," or "homicide." And you can use the weapon or tactic as a variation, too. The victim could be "gunned down," "garroted," "suffocated," "impaled," etc.

One of the few exceptions to this rule is your protagonist's name. It's perfectly acceptable to use it more than once, but even then, you need to limit it. No more than one iteration of the name per paragraph and never two sentences in a row. Use a pronoun or a descriptor like we discussed in Chapter 9.

Homework

Now that you've got a good handle on tone and techniques, go back to the sample blurbs you wrote. Look for areas you can improve them. Ask yourself these questions:

- Do you have genre markers in the text to clearly identify what sort of story this is?
- Could you apply some alliteration or wordplay to better drive home the tone?
- Have you overexplained something?
- Could you trade down some words or use a cliché to simplify?
- Do you have echoes?
- What synonyms could you use to fix them?
- Can you rewrite the sentence, so you don't need the word?

This is the shaping and the crafting of the language to make it sing. This is how you take a basic description and turn it into fine ad copy. Remember: The purpose of a blurb is not to *summarize* the book; it is to *sell* it. In that endeavor, tight, clever copy is the right tool for the job.

CHAPTER 21
CONCLUSION

Congratulations! You've reached the end. But really, this is a beginning. We took a deep dive into the Best Page Forward Way for fantastic fiction blurbs. Now, you're ready to start writing effective book descriptions. Here are some final thoughts to carry you on your way.

Blurb Writing Is Hard

You probably realize this having made it all the way through this intensive. But I don't want to sugarcoat the labor in front of you. Penning great ad copy takes a *lot* of work. Unless you're a natural (and some of us are), this won't come easily.

We built Best Page Forward over a period of six years at the time of this writing. It's the premier ad copy agency in the indie author game. But it's not like we woke up and knew how to do it. Our process has evolved with time. This book is the result of our changed approach from the time our founder, Bryan Cohen, published *How to Write a Sizzling Synopsis.* All that happened because we did the hard work of learning what was effective.

Understand that you *will* have to work at this. You won't be a pro at it overnight. However, you *can* do it. This is a learnable skill that you can master it.

When you're struggling with a turn of phrase, you're not sure which plot elements to include, and it all feels like it's going nowhere, remind yourself that this ain't easy. If you get blocked, instead of stewing in frustration, get up and walk away from it. Let it cook in the back of your mind, then come back refreshed.

Practice Helps

Like anything hard, if you keep with it, you can get better. One of the reasons I had you practice throughout the book on novels or movies you like, is so that you could learn the skills without being personally invested in the material. You may love *The Fast & the Furious*, but writing a blurb for it allows you to work on developing your copywriting abilities without being emotionally tied to the material.

I recommend you spend more time practicing. You're no doubt eager to get to your own work. You've absorbed all the material in these pages, and you've done the exercises. You figure it's time to apply the lessons.

But I'll tell you a secret: It's always going to be harder to write a blurb for your own book. Every single one of us at Best Page Forward fights this battle. We can crank out terrific-sounding copy for our clients and then pull our hair out when it's time to do our own blurbs. The reason is, we're too close to the material. When we're working on a customer's project, we have the advantage of distance. Without that emotional connection to the material or intimate knowledge of the story, it's a lot easier to figure out what should be in there and what should not.

I encourage you to continue practicing on material that is not your own. Not only will it allow you to hone your copywriting skills, but you'll also get better at identifying the inciting incident and the elements of the story that will help it sell.

One of the ways you can do this is to practice each sentence. The gut punch is very different from the complication. Take a movie or book you love and write three versions of each sentence. Try to make them different. How many ways can you get the idea across while still keeping that line short and punchy?

Remember the old joke: "How do you get to Carnegie Hall? Practice, practice, practice."

The Purpose of a Blurb

We'll conclude by bringing you back to the beginning. (Cue "Circle of Life" from *The Lion King*.) We've hit this point over and over throughout the book. Here's your final reminder:

The purpose of a book description is not to summarize the novel; it is to sell it.

If you don't take another thing away from this book, remember this. *Every* choice you make needs to be about getting the sale. When you sit down to write your blurb, you need to stop being the author. Forget that this is something you wrote. Forget that years of your life, of your best memories, of your heart and soul are tied up in it. All that is the author's problem.

When you're writing the description, you're the marketing director. You don't care about what's between the covers. That's not what's going to sell it. Readers want books in genres they enjoy, with main characters they can identify with and root for. They don't care about the plot. They don't care about the themes. They don't care how good the writing is, as long as it doesn't suck. They want a protagonist navigating a relatable conflict in a genre they like.

Write your copy with that in mind. Strip away all the trappings and *sell*.

You can be good at this. You can learn to sell your books as well as you write them. You can make your indie author dreams come true.

I look forward to reading your blurbs.

* * *

Love blurb writing but need to get this task off your plate? Hate blurb writing and want someone else to take care of it for you? Scan the QR code below to order a done-for-you book description from our team instantly!

Want to get advice on your rewritten blurbs? Scan the QR code below to join our year-round Facebook community of authors at Selling for Authors.

ABOUT THE AUTHORS

Phoebe J. Ravencraft is the Editor-in-Chief of Best Page Forward, an award-winning game designer, and an independent author of paranormal women's fiction and urban fantasy. She's been a business and marketing copywriter for 25 years and a recovering English major for even longer. She still geeks out over a well-crafted turn of phrase.

When she's not penning blurbs or novels about strong women wielding supernatural power, Phoebe plays *Magic: The Gathering* and binges Netflix. She lives with a dog and a cat whose sole mission in life is to interrupt her Zoom meetings.

Bryan Cohen is the CEO of Best Page Forward, and author copywriting agency that has written over 5,000 book descriptions for the author community. He's also an author who has sold 140,000+ copies of his novels and nonfiction. Each quarter, he runs the 5-Day Author Ad Profit Challenge, an event that helps authors create more profitable ads.

He lives with his wife, daughter, and cat in sunny North Carolina.

Go to BestPageForward.net/blurbs to order your book description package today!

APPENDIX A: HOMEWORK ASSIGNMENTS

If you're one of those people who likes to wait until the end to do the homework, here is a summary of all the assignments for your convenience.

Exercise 1: Stakes and Inciting Incident

Pick one-five of your favorite novels or films (mix and match, if you like). For each one:

1. Determine who the main character is. For romance you can pick two

2. Name the stakes for the MC

3. Determine the inciting incident

Exercise 2: The Protagonist's Emotional Journey

For each of your chosen movies or books, identify the main character's emotional journey through the story. Figure out what the story is really about.

Then, write one sentence for each film/novel. Write a transition phrase that gives background or plot information from the story and a main clause that reveals the main character's emotional state or journey.

Exercise 3: Agency

Pick an important scene from each film/novel that you think you would include if you were writing a blurb. Write a sentence for each one describing it, making sure to give the protagonist agency. Remember:

- Make them the subject of the sentence
- Wherever possible, use a dynamic, powerful verb
- Avoid using forms of "must"

Exercise 4: The MC's Perspective

For each movie/novel ask yourself, "What is the main character's emotional journey?" Forget the plots for a moment. What emotions are the protagonists experiencing or struggling with?

Now, write two sentences for each novel or film. In both of them, focus on writing from inside the character's perspective. Look out through their eyes at the world instead of down on them from above.

Use emotionally charged words, especially verbs, to describe this person's journey. Let the reader see what they are feeling.

Exercise 5: Editing Language

By now, you should have a number of sample blurb sentences from your chosen movies/books. Pick out a few of them and practice editing. Make sure:

- They are in third-person present tense
- Check to see if the MC has agency
- Are we inside the protagonist's head looking out?
- Ensure that the strongest idea is at the end

Exercise 6: Picking the Right Content

Go back to the books/films you've been working on each chapter. For now, treat them as single POV, even if they are romances. Pick out the main character or the most-main character. Then, determine what the content should be for each sentence in the blurb. You don't need to worry about actually writing those out. Just make a note of what you believe needs to be in each sentence.

If you get stuck, identify the inciting incident. Put that in P1S3 and work backwards to the start of the story. Likewise, figure out what a major complication is and put that in P2S2. For P2S1, ask yourself what would go between that and the inciting incident.

Exercise 7: Writing The Hook

Go back to your chosen films/novels and write three hooks for each – a one-sentence, a two-sentence, and a three-sentence. Remember that each should provide the answer to three questions:

- What does the main character want?
- What is standing in their way?
- What are the consequences of failure?

End on the strongest concept, the highest possible stakes, and whenever possible, the strongest word.

Exercise 8: Writing The Gut Punch

Write a P1S1 for each of your chosen movies/books. Remember to:

- Keep it to six to ten words
- Eliminate the plot and focus solely on the character's strongest emotion
- Stay in the MC's POV

Exercise 9: Writing The Expansion

Write an expansion for each of your chosen films/books, remembering to do the following:

- Stay inside the MC's perspective
- Keep agency with the protagonist
- Use the past to reveal the present
- Use the plot/background to reveal emotion
- Raise the emotional stakes

Exercise 10: Writing The Inciting Incident

Look at the work you did for Exercise 1. Now that you have a clearer distinction between the story's opening events and its inciting incident, did you identify the correct plot point for each book or movie? If so, great! If not, take a moment to figure out what it actually is.

With your chosen inciting incidents lined up, write a P1S3 for each film or novel. Remember that:

- It is an external story event
- That acts on the protag
- Forcing them into the action of the narrative

But when we write that sentence, we want to:

- Remain inside the protagonist's head
- Focus on showing the MC's emotional reaction to the inciting incident
- Give the main character agency

AND:

- Threaten the protagonist's status quo
- End on the highest possible stakes
- Push readers over the fold

Exercise 11: Writing The Bridge

Write a Bridge for each movie or novel. Experiment with using the traditional order and the reversed version. Remember our goals:

- Use plot to reveal the MC's new emotional state
- Re-hook the reader, so they don't navigate away
- Keep the agency with the protagonist

Exercise 12: Writing The Complication

What's a major complication that's standing in the way of the main character in each of your chosen novels or films? There are probably several. Choose one that occurs roughly in the first half of the story but definitely has an impact on the outcome.

Now, write those P2S2s. Don't forget to end on the highest possible stakes and make them personal.

Exercise 13: Writing The Cliffhanger

Write a cliffhanger for each of your chosen movies or books. Don't forget to:

- Pose it as a question
- Ask if the hero will succeed
- Raise the stakes to the highest they can possibly go
- Set it off from P2 in its own paragraph

Exercise 14: Writing The Selling Paragraph

This exercise might be a little trickier than the others if you're using movies or if all the samples you chose are standalones. If you're working on a film, pretend it's a book for this assignment. If you don't have any series choices, act like one of them is, make up a series name for it, and do the exercise that way.

Your task is to go through your chosen books/movies and write selling paragraphs for each one. Remember:

- The first sentence tells the reader what it is
- Book/movie name
- Which number in the series it is
- The name of the series

- What genre it is
- The second sentence tells the reader why they'll like it
- Name three tropes that feature in the story
- Name the author (or director for a film)

Exercise 15: Writing The CTA

Write a call to action for each of your chosen films/books. Even if you plan to never use the clever-phrase portion of the BPF CTA formula, experiment with doing it here. It will help you practice your copywriting skills.

Exercise 16: 2-POV Blurbs

Romance authors, this is your moment. I'm betting at least one of those books or films you chose was actually a romance. Throw out your P2 and craft a proper 2-POV blurb for it.

If you didn't choose a romance for any of your exercises, take a look at your choices. Is there one where there's a strong secondary character you could use? If not, here are a few examples you could pick for this exercise that have two main characters but are not romance:

- *Toy Story* (Woody and Buzz)
- *Frozen* (Anna and Elsa)
- *Lethal Weapon* (Riggs and Murtaugh)
- *Bill & Ted's Excellent Adventure* (Bill and Ted)
- *Gilmore Girls* (Lorelei and Rory)

You can probably think of a few others if you don't like any of those or are unfamiliar with all of them. The point is, select a story that has two driving characters and give them each a POV paragraph and then a P3 with two complications.

Exercise 17: Memoir Blurbs

Pick your favorite memoir. Try writing a blurb for it. Remember that it needs to contain all the elements a fiction description does – especially an inciting incident. Add the explanation paragraph to capture the feel of the book, so the reader has a clear idea what they'll be getting.

Exercise 18: Tuning and Editing

Go back to the sample blurbs you wrote. Look for areas you can improve them. Ask yourself these questions:

- Do you have genre markers in the text to clearly identify what sort of story this is?
- Could you apply some alliteration or wordplay to better drive home the tone?
- Have you overexplained something?
- Could you trade down some words or use a cliché to simplify?
- Do you have echoes?
- What synonyms could you use to fix them?
- Can you rewrite the sentence so you don't need the word?

This is the shaping and the crafting of the language to make it sing. This is how you take a basic description and turn it into really fine ad copy. Remember: The purpose of a blurb is not to *summarize* the book; it is to *sell* it. In that endeavor, tight, clever copy is the right tool for the job.

APPENDIX B: BEST PAGE FORWARD BLURB TEMPLATES

Standard Fiction Blurb Template

Most book descriptions walk this path. They follow the early emotional journey of a single main character in this exact fashion:

The Hook

P1S1: *The Gut Punch*

P1S2: *The Expansion*

P1S3: *The Inciting Incident*

P2S1: *The Bridge*

P2S2: *The Complication*

The Cliffhanger

The Selling Paragraph

The Call to Action (CTA)

The 2-POV Fiction Blurb Template

If you're a romance author, you know you have to talk about both of the lovers in the story. You essentially have two main characters, who both need equal time.

Some other types of novels benefit from this as well. Literary fiction, women's fiction, and books with parallel narratives sometimes do better with a second POV in the blurb. In those cases, we use the template below:

The Hook

P1S1: *The Gut Punch*

P1S2: *The Expansion*

P1S3: *The Inciting Incident*

P2S1: *The Uppercut*

P2S2: *The Inciting Incident (Again)*

P2S3: *The Consequence*

P3S1: *The First Complication*

P3S2: *The Second Complication*

The Cliffhanger

The Selling Paragraph

The Call to Action

The Memoir Blurb Template

Depending on how much material you want to include, you can either go with one or two paragraphs for the main body of the blurb before adding an explainer paragraph.

The Hook

P1S1: *The Gut Punch*

P1S2: *The Expansion*

P1S3: *The Inciting Incident*

P2S1: *The Bridge*

P2S2: *The Complication*

P3S1: *The Explanation*

P3S2: *The Story*

P3S3: *The Benefit*

The Selling Paragraph

The Call to Action

* * *

Scan the QR code below to order a done-for-you book description from our team instantly!

Made in the USA
Middletown, DE
26 August 2022

72302950R00106